# VICTORY ON THE HOME FRONT

## A WORLD WAR II STORY

*While Her Husband Fought, She Built Planes ~ She was a Rosie the Riveter*

LILLY ROBBINS BROCK

**VICTORY ON THE HOME FRONT**



Official Website: **http://www.lillyrobbinsbrock.com**

# TABLE OF CONTENTS

DEDICATION .......... V
PROLOGUE .......... VII
CHAPTER 1 .......... 1
CHAPTER 2 .......... 5
CHAPTER 3 .......... 19
CHAPTER 4 .......... 25
CHAPTER 5 .......... 27
CHAPTER 6 .......... 29
CHAPTER 7 .......... 35
CHAPTER 8 .......... 41
CHAPTER 9 .......... 45
CHAPTER 10 .......... 55
CHAPTER 11 .......... 59
CHAPTER 12 .......... 67
CHAPTER 13 .......... 71
CHAPTER 14 .......... 79
CHAPTER 15 .......... 85
CHAPTER 16 .......... 87
CHAPTER 17 .......... 89
CHAPTER 18 .......... 105
ACKNOWLEDGMENTS .......... 107
REFERENCES .......... 109
AUTHOR'S NOTE TO READERS .......... 113
AUTHOR BIO .......... 115

# Dedication

To my parents and all those who were part of the Greatest Generation.

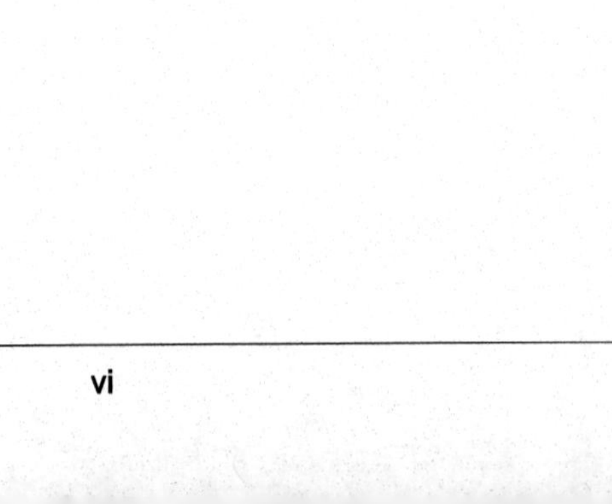

# Prologue

As a baby boomer, I've always felt a strong connection to the Greatest Generation. My parents were part of that generation. My dad served in World War II, and shortly after he returned from the war, he met my mother. They married in June 1947, and in March 1948, boom—I was born. I often teased my mother, and said, "Mom, I did the math. I must have been a honeymoon baby?" She replied in a very serious tone, "Of course, don't think for a moment that anything happened before we were married!" Both my parents are gone now, and I miss them terribly.

There are still people from the Greatest Generation living among us, and their stories need to be told. I think of these people as treasures. I've recently written two life story books thus far—*Wooden Boats & Iron Men* and *Ever A Soldier*. As I've gone on book tours with these books, I've met many people who have a loved one from that generation. They always tell me, "Nothing has been written down." I emphatically encourage them to at least use a tape recorder to get their loved one's words on tape. Their words can always be transcribed into a story later. Once these treasured people are gone, their stories go with them forever.

The idea of writing about a Rosie the Riveter actually piqued in October of 2012 while I was on a genealogy mission. I wanted to become a member of the Daughters of the American Revolution. To qualify, I needed hard evidence of my direct family connection to each past generation leading to my patriot who served in the Revolutionary War. I had already spent countless hours breaking through a brick wall of my great grandfather on my dad's side. Through hours of detective work, I discovered our family had important roots in Ypsilanti, Michigan, and it was where I would find the answers I needed. No one in the family had ever known about Ypsilanti.

Off I flew to Ypsilanti. I donned my detective hat and spent ten days uncovering information, which had been buried for decades. Ypsi, the affectionate name used by the locals, is a small town, so I spent much of my time on foot—literally walking in my ancestors' footsteps. Many of the historic buildings that line the streets of Ypsi have been there since the 1800s. I even tracked down the address of my great uncle's business, which had been in one of the commercial buildings. As I walked through the town and the residential neighborhoods, I thought, if only these old buildings could talk. I found the stately old church my ancestors had attended, and I visualized them walking up the steps and entering the building through the massive carved doors.

There were areas outside of town I needed to explore as well, so I rented a car. On one particular day, I ventured out to the rural area and found my great-great grandfather's farm. After feeling quite successful with my find, I proceeded to head back to town, but took the wrong road, and got lost. In those days, I didn't have a smart phone, thus, no navigation.

I ended up on a pot-holed semi-paved road with grass growing through the cracks, which led me to an old vacant factory building. It sat eerily quiet, and it was black as night inside. Daylight was fading, and there weren't any streetlights. I shined my headlights toward the building, and saw a faded sign near it, which read, Willow Run Factory. I knew I had discovered something important from the past, and I had to know more.

After finally finding my way back to town in the dark, I was most anxious to return to the hotel and ask some questions. I learned that the factory had been built by the Ford Motor Company to fulfill the need to build the B-24 bomber plane, (known as the Liberator), for World War II. That night in my room, I stayed up for hours researching the Willow Run Factory on my laptop.

The factory began production in 1942. Using Henry Ford's mass production technology, the factory produced one B-24 every fifty-five minutes. Forty-two thousand people worked at the factory, and one-third of them were women. It was at Willow Run where the original Rosie the Riveter icon began.

Somehow, I felt a connection to the lonely abandoned factory. Maybe it was because I had come to know Ypsi so intimately. By now, I felt qualified to refer to the town as Ypsi. I had even met five long-lost cousins who lived there. One cousin was ninety-five years old. Maybe some of my family had worked in the factory. Maybe, it was because my father was a World War II veteran. All I knew was that I was drawn to it.

Tears came to my eyes when I learned the factory was doomed to the wrecking ball the following year, 2013. I went back to look at the factory one last time before leaving Ypsi. In my mind, the spirit of all the Rosie the Riveters lingered in the building. I told myself that one day I must write about a Rosie the Riveter.

Fortunately, there were people, including myself, who didn't want to see the demise of this historical relic. As scheduled, the demolition process began in the fall of 2013, and continued into 2014. In an effort to save a portion of the plant that was still standing, the Michigan Aerospace Foundation and the Yankee Air Museum formed Save the Willow Run Bomber Plant campaign. Their goal was to raise eight million dollars to buy 144,000 square feet of the bomber plant before the deadline of May 1, 2014. The campaign became known as Save Rosie's Factory, and was in commemoration of the women who contributed to the World

War II effort. They achieved their goal. I'm proud to admit that I donated to this cause.

I've kept tabs on this project. At the moment, it's projected that by early next year, 2018, the restored and renovated bomber plant will become the National Museum of Aviation & Technology at Historic Willow Run.

* * *

Five years later, 2017, I met Priscilla Messinger, an actual Rosie the Riveter, who lives in Kelso, Washington, just a few miles away from me. Now, I'm writing her story.

The story has expanded, however. As Priscilla talked about her life, I learned about her husband, Dean. He was a World War II veteran—a fighting Seabee. How could I write about her and not write about him? This is no longer a story solely abut a Rosie the Riveter, but the story of a young married couple separated by World War II. So many marriages were put on hold. As husbands fought overseas, wives built the machines they needed to win the war.

"We are our stories. We tell them to stay alive or keep alive those who only live now in the telling."

~Niall Williams—*History of the Rain*

# Chapter 1

"There is one front and one battle where everyone in the United States—every man, woman, and child—is in action, and will be privileged to remain in action throughout this war. That front is right here at home, in our daily tasks."

~President Franklin D. Roosevelt, April 28th, 1942

Priscilla and Dean were married just over a year when the Japanese Empire attacked Pearl Harbor on Sunday, December 7, 1941. Their life was about to change.

The war had been raging in Europe since 1939. President Roosevelt tried to avoid involving the United States in the war, and even promised the American people he wouldn't send their loved ones off to fight. His promise was snatched away when the Japanese engaged in a sneak attack on Pearl Harbor on that infamous day, killing 2,403 Americans and wounding another 1,178. On December 11th, Hitler and Nazi Germany declared war on the United States, and on the same day, the United States declared war on Germany and Italy.

The newlyweds knew it was only a matter of time before Dean would be called to serve. At the time, men between the ages of eighteen and thirty-five were drafted. Many men felt compelled to volunteer to defend their country. A year and a half later, Dean joined the Navy, and applied to train for a new kind of soldier—a Seabee.

The Seabees were formed to fill an urgent need.

Before the Japanese took control of the Pacific islands, the United States had sent several hundred civilian workers to the islands to improve the living conditions. After the Pearl Harbor attack, the Japanese took control of one Pacific island after another, and upon seizing the island, captured the American construction workers. Without any defensive training or weaponry, the workers were easy prey.

Recognizing the urgency to build and defend, the concept of the first naval construction company, the 130th Battalion, emerged in December 1941. By September of 1943, the 130th Battalion became a reality. Men from all walks of life stepped up for training.

Following is a quote from the book, *U.S. Navy Seabee Museum, One Hundred and Thirtieth U.S. Naval Construction,* by the U.S. Naval Construction Battalion, 130th.

"We were insurance men, grocers, welders, merchants, accountants, architects, bakers, butchers, brick masons, mailmen, machinists, dining car stewards, teachers, salesmen. We came from the north and from the south, and more than one-third of us were from the metropolitan areas of Illinois, New York, Pennsylvania, and Massachusetts."

* * *

In the year 1943, a film was made about the Seabees, which was released in early 1944. It was called *The Fighting Seabees,* starring John Wayne and Susan Hayward. The film brought so much attention to the feats and heroism of the Seabees, the name *Seabees* became a household name until the end of the war.

* * *

Dean was among the first to join the Seabees. He had worked for a construction company in Longview, Washington, and on

July 9, 1943, his boss sent a letter of recommendation to the U.S. Navy Construction Battalion recruiting office. Dean was accepted and inducted on July 27, 1943, with the date of entry as August 4th of the 130th Battalion, Company D, 5th Platoon. The Battalion was official the following month, and Dean was ready to start training. His Battalion would be attached to the 4th Division Marine Corps.

The month of August began with Priscilla and Dean standing in the train station. Like so many other emotional couples gathered there, oblivious to those around them, they clung to each other up to the final moment until the train whistle signaled the hour of departure. The station was crowded with couples saying farewell.

"It was a tearful scene. I was sad and crying, but I was trying not to make it harder for him," said Priscilla.

The heartache of wartime goodbyes was a common theme. A soldier comforted his girl as she wept. He dabbed her tears with his handkerchief and pulled her in close with her chin resting on his shoulder. Other couples clenched hands and chattered nervously about their plans when they would be together again. Each ignoring the possibility he may not return, and this could be their final goodbye.

After one last embrace, Dean and the other warriors boarded the train. While the train chugged slowly, then faster, out of the station, some soldiers hung out the windows with eyes locked on the ones they were leaving behind. Their tear-filled eyes said it all—sadness, fear, and tender love. When the train picked up speed, some of those left behind ran alongside the train to wave as long as possible. Once the train was out of view, the silence in the train station was deafening, and the wives, sweethearts, mothers, family members, and friends reluctantly left the station to try to resume their lives.

As she watched her husband leave, Priscilla realized she was suddenly a single mother of a five-month-old baby. She was on her own, and she didn't know for how long. As a wife and mother, she was forced to put her married life on hold until, most likely, the end of the war. *How long will this war last?*

She chose to ignore the question lurking in the deepest recess of her mind—*Will he come back?* Life was going to be different now.

After Priscilla left the train station, she drove to the home of her brother and sister-in-law to pick up her baby girl, Carol Ann. They had volunteered to care for her while Priscilla was seeing Dean off. For the first time, it was just her and Carol Ann.

When they arrived home, Priscilla opened the door to a quiet and empty house. She wouldn't be cooking dinner for her and Dean that night. She wouldn't be enjoying conversation with him over a cup of coffee the following morning, and several mornings thereafter. *How many mornings would she drink coffee alone?* When she opened the closet door, his clothes hung idle all neatly lined up as he had left them, and his scent still lingered in the air. She thought about how Dean would miss all the *firsts* of their baby girl. She had promised to write to him daily and to send pictures. He promised to do the same, if he could.

# Chapter 2

Priscilla thought back to another time in her life when she was alone. It was during her senior year in high school. Those years had been a bittersweet time in her life. Fate had stepped in, and brought happiness and sadness. Since her marriage to Dean, her life had been moving in a fast forward pace.

After Priscilla put Carol Ann to bed at night, and the house was quiet, she often ruminated about her life. She reflected on the three communities that played a part in her being—Aloha, Pacific Beach, and Moclips, each interwoven into her life. On some of those lonely nights, she couldn't help but think about her mother who had been in a similar situation, unexpectedly left alone. In fact, she was the third generation of women in her family who had to survive on their own.

* * *

It's a mystery how Margaret, Priscilla's mother, ended up in the small logging town of Aloha, Washington by herself. Margaret Evelyn Dayton had lived in Minnesota until 1903. Margaret was a young girl when her father left his wife and child. Her mother claimed abandonment on the divorce papers—her father had joined Roosevelt's Rough Riders to fight in the Spanish American War.

Margaret's mother, Larinda, earned a sparse living working as a servant in a boarding house. One day, she answered a newspaper ad asking for a ranch cook in Baker,

Montana. After landing the job, she mustered up her courage, packed their few belongings, and she and ten-year-old Margaret boarded a train headed to Montana.

Margaret and her mother were among throngs of people moving to Montana for a chance of a better life. Montana experienced a homestead boom, and the town of Baker had quickly become a boomtown. The government gave away millions of acres of land, and the railroad companies sent out posters and ads across the nation, and as far away as Europe, advertising free green fertile farmland in Montana. The rains had turned Montana into a green paradise.

When Margaret was about seventeen, she met a Montana cowboy by the name of Erving Dean (full name, Robert Erving Dean). They married on April 20, 1910, in Bowman, North Dakota, which was only a few miles past the Montana-North Dakota line.

By 1912, Margaret gave birth to a son, named Mourland, and two years later, 1914, gave birth to their second son, Myron.

* * *

The year 1917 brought unexpected changes to the people of Montana.

The United States entered World War I joining its allies—Britain, France and Russia. Food was needed overseas, and the government pushed farmers to increase production to meet the demands of the war. The government also encouraged the farmers to borrow money to buy additional farm equipment such as tractors, threshers, and plows. There was a slogan—*Food Will Win The War*. The farmers felt they were performing their patriotic duty as they plunged into debt.

The homesteaders felt that they had settled into a green paradise. The weather conditions seemed perfect with an annual rainfall of fifteen to eighteen inches a year keeping everything green and fertile. They felt confident to forge ahead, and in the process, transformed the Montana landscape. They built houses, roads, and towns, and strung fences for grazing livestock. They hunted the game animals until they nearly disappeared. They plowed thousands of acres for cropland, but when they plowed the land, they destroyed the native grasslands. The grasslands not only held the soil, but also held the moisture in the soil.

The homesteaders were unaware of Montana's alternating weather cycles. There were years of rain, and then years of drought. In 1917, the drought years returned. Rainfall was less than ten inches that year, and temperatures soared to one hundred degrees. The hot dry winds shriveled the crops, and since the homesteaders' plowing techniques loosened the soil and destroyed the vegetation, the wind lifted the loose dirt, resulting in dust storms. The dust made it difficult to breathe outside, as well as inside as it blew its way into the buildings. The water sources dried up, and livestock died. Then came the prairie fires and the locusts.

Suddenly, the farmers who had become successful were thrown into poverty. They hoped the drought would only last for the year, but the next year was worse.

Like so many other people trying to survive during these conditions, Margaret and Erving made plans to leave Montana.

The following year, Margaret found herself on her own in Aloha. It is unknown how she heard about the town or who she knew there.

She wrote a letter to her husband dated June 26, 1918.

*Dear Hubby, how are you getting along? Is Sadie (his sister) there or are you batching? ...We went out to the Pacific Beach last night with one of the Bossess. They have a new Buick car. It is only two miles from here with the ocean. I thot it was the sound they were near but it is the ocean itself. It is just beautiful.... It is quite pretty here but I don't know if I would like to live here or not, there are not flowers at all here....There are about forty to fifty soldiers working in the mill and we are going up to see them drill tomorrow night.*

*I don't believe I could stay a month if I tried so look for me soon.*

*Well good bye*

*I am as ever your*

*Loving Margaret.*

Margaret returned to Montana by the end of the summer. By the following year, she and Erving and their two sons moved to Aloha. The 1920 census shows Margaret employed by the Aloha Lumber Company. She had taken a job at the Aloha Lumber Company in the position of an off-bearer at the re-saw. There is a picture of her standing with a group of men at the mill, dated 1919. Later, she transitioned to the position as a cook for the loggers. Erving worked for the mill as a tree faller.

The 1920 census also shows Margaret's mother and stepfather, Erving's parents and sister, his brother and wife, and other family members living in Aloha, Washington. The entire family had lived in Fallon County, Montana, and moved together to Aloha. The family was happy to be living in green country again, plus by driving the short distance to the nearby communities of Moclips and Pacific Beach, they had easy access to the Pacific Ocean, and everything it offered.

Had Margaret's 1918 sojourn to the lumber mill been a few months earlier, she would have encountered some horrendous working conditions and experienced, first hand, the drama of angry loggers on strike for a better living.

The living conditions in the Pacific Northwest logging camps were abominable. The food was barely edible and kept in unsanitary conditions such as raw meat covered with flies. The open toilet pits were situated too close to sleeping quarters and/or the cooking area, the bunkhouses didn't have beds, and the bedrolls were damp or rain soaked and infested with fleas. The biggest complaint from the loggers was about the requirement of having to work as long as there was daylight, which in the spring and summer months resulted in ten to fourteen-hour days. Despite the loggers' complaints to the mill owners, nothing improved. The loggers felt they had no choice, and joined an organization called the Industrial Workers of the World (IWW). Members were called Wobblies. By the summer of 1917, IWW organized a series of strikes, which spread throughout the Pacific Northwest, demanding improved conditions for the loggers, especially an eight-hour day. The owners were vehemently against the reduction in hours since they paid the men by the day rather than by the hour. They were defiantly resistant to the demands.

As World War I raged on, the factory and logging company owners looked forward to the surplus profit they expected to receive, but they had no plans of sharing it with their workers. The European Allies had discovered that the Sitka spruce species of wood was ideal for building airplanes needed for the war, and this species grew in the Pacific Northwest. They requested one hundred million board feet of aeroplane stock. With the demand for the increase of air power for the Allies to fight the war, the market price per board foot doubled, and doubled again.

All was not well, however, for the logging industry owners. After the IWW entered the picture, loggers continued to strike, and were encouraged to sabotage equipment. Fighting broke out, and production slowed dramatically, which didn't go unnoticed by the U.S. Army. The Army had formed the Spruce Production Division (SPD), a part of the U.S. Army Signal Corps, to increase the production of airplane wood by providing men and equipment. They sent a retired general by the name of Brice Disque to investigate the situation, and to provide a quick solution to the labor problems. He was given command of the newly formed SPD.

While Disque recognized the Wobs had legitimate complaints, he also realized the armed Wobs, which by now had a membership of one hundred thousand members, had become a volatile and dangerous organization. The mill owners weren't budging, and neither were the Wobblies.

Disque had a plan. In the fall of 1917, he organized the Loyal Legion of Loggers & Lumbermen (LLLL). In December, he sent SPD Signal Corps officers out to the lumber camps, mills, and mill towns to recruit members for the Four-L. It became an army unit of men to fight in the woods of the Pacific Northwest rather than the trenches in France. Each man took a loyalty oath, and could not be a member of the IWW. Every soldier had to join the Four-L as well as the managers of the mills and camps. With the presence of the Four-L, the IWW slowly declined.

Disque offered mill owners a solution with a promise to end the strikes, and to increase production. At the time, mill labor had lowered to fifteen percent. He offered to place Army troops in the logging camps to work alongside the civilian workers. This appealed to the mill owners. They had been losing money, and losing their opportunity to make tremendous profits. They could apply for troop labor, but not without agreeing to a full list of requirements, which included proper working and living conditions for the workers, and the core issue—agreeing to an eight-hour day. Soldiers could be available by January 1, 1918.

By May 2, 1918, sixty-two logging operations in Washington and Oregon had soldiers working side by side with their civilian workers. Aloha Lumber Company was one of the participants. Because of the SPD program, the strikes and anger ended, and the loggers could expect a bunkhouse with heat when needed, clean bedding, sanitary toilets, showers, decent food, and an eight-hour workday.

Between the men who were in the fight overseas, and the recent strikes, the mills had experienced a labor shortage. They were under pressure to fulfill their contract with the government to provide the much needed airplane wood for the European Allies. They needed workers, and by May, several soldiers were added to their workforce. These were the soldiers that Margaret saw, and spoke about in her letter to her husband, Erving.

Margaret had entered an important moment in logging history. Had it not been for the war, she most likely wouldn't have been hired for a position normally held by a man.

Margaret Dean (Priscilla's mother) working at Aloha Lumber Co., 1919

Margaret Dean (Priscilla's mother) working at Aloha Lumber Co., 1919

* * *

By January of 1922, Margaret was pregnant with their third child, Priscilla. While she was carrying Priscilla, sadly, their oldest son, Mourland, died at the age of ten from a brain tumor. Priscilla was born on September 14$^{th}$, which happened to be on her brother Myron's eighth birthday. At first, he was displeased—he had hoped for a brother. Once he adjusted to having a little sister, he became a loving and protective brother.

Priscilla's life evolved around the lumber industry. While her father worked in the woods as a tree faller, her mother cooked for fifteen loggers. Her brother also worked in the woods. The mill company owners provided housing throughout the town for the residents. "They owned the entire town," said Priscilla. The men either worked at the local saw mill or commuted to the logging site on the speeder.

The Dean family lived in a single level house, which had enough bedrooms to allow the Deans to take in boarders. The loggers lived nearby in an adjacent bunkhouse.

Every morning, Priscilla's mother, Margaret, arose early to prepare breakfast for the loggers, which she served at 6:00 a.m. Breakfast included eggs, bacon, ham, toast, muffins, and fresh fruit. A large pitcher of milk was always on the table. When the loggers arrived for breakfast, the aroma of coffee welcomed them. They ate fast and didn't talk. The night before, Margaret prepared lunchboxes for the loggers. Lunch consisted of meat sandwiches, boiled eggs, fruit, cookies, and doughnuts. "My father and I always helped her. We worked late into the night," said Priscilla. When the loggers finished their breakfast, each man picked up his lunchbox and headed for the speeder for the ride to the woods. At the end of the eight-hour workday, the mill whistle blew, and the speeder brought the loggers back to town where they filed into the boarding house for a hefty supper. The loggers looked forward to supper. A typical supper included some kind of meat, potatoes and gravy, biscuits, vegetables, fruit, and dessert, such as pie, cake, doughnuts, pudding or custards. As usual, a pitcher of milk accompanied the meal. The loggers required an enormous amount of food, averaging eight to nine thousand calories a day in order to have enough stamina for the workday ahead.

When Priscilla wasn't in school, she helped her mother. "I set the table and helped her serve the food. Then I cleared the table. Mother was an excellent cook and a hard worker."

The Dean home on Front Street, #13, in Aloha, from 1920

* * *

Priscilla's only sibling was her older brother, Myron. When she was in grade school, her folks decided she needed a sister. "My parents were very kind people. They knew about an orphan girl who lived in Seattle. She had experienced a rough life. Her mother had died, and she was passed from one person to another. Her father was never around. They decided to take her in and make her part of the family. Her name was Gladys. We might as well have been sisters. We became very close, and we stayed in touch through our marital years."

* * *

Priscilla's parents celebrated their twenty-fifth wedding anniversary with friends on April 19, 1935. The Aloha newspaper reported the social event,

*Aloha, April 24 – Mr. And Mrs. Robert E. Dean of Aloha celebrated their 25th wedding anniversary Friday evening, April 19, at the Aloha Hall with an old-fashioned dance. R.B. Harper and Fred Harper furnished the music. An amusing feature of the evening was a burlesque wedding ceremony, with Alex Smith taking the part of the bride's father, typifying the rural mountaineer who used persuasion on the groom at the end of an antiquated shotgun. Paul Bryn, acting as the parson, performed a lengthy ceremony.*

*Mr. And Mrs. Dean were married at Bowman, North Dakota,*

*April 20, 1910, and for the past 16 years have resided at Aloha. Mrs. Dean was formerly Miss Margaret Dayton. Those who attended were …*

* * *

Priscilla was active in high school. She was in the school orchestra and played the violin, and she was a member of the girls' baseball and basketball teams. If she wasn't participating in a game, Priscilla and her friends cheered the boys' teams on. Sometimes they rode the bus to an out-of-town game to support the players.

The young people of Aloha found many ways to entertain themselves. They went to dances, the skating rink, parties, and swam in the ocean at Pacific Beach. They watched the latest movies at Aloha Hall and enjoyed ice cream afterwards at the local cafe. If they weren't out and about, they gathered at each other's houses and listened to the radio, or played Chinese Checkers or Fiddle-Sticks.

Life in Aloha wasn't only about logging. The townspeople believed in enjoying life. They worked hard and played hard.

* * *

Priscilla started a diary in 1936 and kept it up until 1940.

She wrote about a night in 1936 when her parents drove to Hoquiam, which was about nineteen miles away to see a movie. It was Will Roger's last picture to be released—*In Old Kentucky*. He had died tragically in a plane crash in Alaska in August 1935. Twentieth Century Fox was uncertain whether to release the picture posthumously, but decided to gamble and release it. The picture was well received. Her parents enjoyed the movie and a night out.

One of Priscilla's fondest memories was a day in June of the same year, when she received a .22 rifle and five boxes of shells as a gift from her father's friend, Ole, who was also a logger. She was turning fourteen. The rifle had been purchased from Montgomery Ward for sixteen dollars. She became a sharpshooter, and earned membership in the Woman's Sharpshooter Club of Cowlitz County, Squad #34, on May 5, 1942.

Priscilla's .22 rifle

Priscilla noted in her diary in 1937 about a movie she went to see and enjoyed. It was called *My Man Godfrey*. Admission was ten cents.

On October 1, 1937, she wrote about witnessing President Roosevelt's historic visit to Aberdeen. It was a special event in her life.

The President was on a mission. He toured the Olympic Peninsula loop from Lake Crescent to Lake Quinault, and visited the cities of Aberdeen and Hoquiam. It was a rainy tour. His son and several grandchildren accompanied him. Priscilla was one of fifty thousand people to greet the president that day.

The purpose of the President's trip was to see the area firsthand and to hear arguments for and against the proposed national park on the peninsula. He announced his support for the park, and signed the bill on June 29, 1938, nine months later, making the Olympic National Park a reality.

Penny had no idea how this ironic event would affect her family in the very near future. Both sets of her grandparents, the Deans and the Rowleys, had homesteaded in Queets on the Olympic Peninsula circa 1935. Through hard work and perseverance, the homesteaders worked their land and had become completely self-sufficient.

Now that the Olympic Peninsula was a national park, the homesteaders were forced to sell their land to the government at a discounted price. Because the Queets was a late addition to the Park, the Queets homesteaders were the last to be forced out. Their time ran out in 1940, when the federal government acquisitioned the Queets Corridor, and condemned the land, forcing the inhabitants to sell out. Priscilla's grandmother, Addie Dean, was now a widow, and moved to Pacific Beach with her son, Lyndon. The Rowley grandparents moved to Aberdeen.

* * *

Aloha is located on the Pacific Coast of the Olympic Peninsula, which is two miles east of the Pacific Ocean. R.D. Emerson and W.H. Dole founded it in 1905. Since the Dole family owned land and conducted business in Hawaii, they named the town Aloha after the Hawaiian greeting. Before long, the small town of Aloha became the home of the Aloha Lumber Company. Then, in 1920, the company won a bid on a unit of untouched timber located near the coastal town of Moclips, just six miles from the Aloha mill.

In 1922, after fighting heavy winter rains for two years, the company succeeded in the construction of a railroad to the Moclips timber site. Besides using the railroad to move logs from the woods to the mill, the company transported the loggers who lived in Aloha to and from the timber site with the use of a steam railway motorcar, called a *speeder*. No one ever wanted to see the speeder come back from the timber site to Aloha off schedule, it meant there had been an accident.

Priscilla explained, "When the speeder showed up unexpectedly, the women in town gathered at the rail stop to learn who had been injured or killed. The women waited fearfully to see who was carried out on a stretcher."

* * *

The nearby coastal town of Moclips sits along the Pacific Ocean and is situated south of the Quinault Indian Nation, three miles northwest of Aloha. The town was incorporated in

1905 when the Northern Pacific Railroad was completed making Moclips its farthest west terminus point. The railroad was a boon to the town. Moclips was the center for manufacturing cedar shingles and shakes, and the railroad made it possible for the mills to transport their products to buyers. Logs could now be moved without depending on water-based transportation. A train depot was built soon thereafter, which accommodated thousands of vacationers who were attracted to Moclips by the sea. It was easy for people to hop on the train and enjoy a day trip to the long stretch of sandy beaches. They picnicked, played and fished in the pounding surf, dug for razor clams, or simply sunk their toes into the wet sand and strolled along the beach.

* * *

Pacific Beach is a close neighbor to Moclips. It was settled in 1863, and started out as a sawmill town, but with its wide-open Pacific Coast beach, it evolved into a well-known resort destination. Like Moclips, it was considered a seaside hotspot.

A large hotel called the Pacific Beach Hotel was built along the bluff in 1906, which became known as the *Honeymoon Hotel*. The hotel prospered until, on the morning of October 3, 1914, a fire broke out and destroyed the structure. The owner, Carl Cooper, used the insurance money to rebuild a more modern, larger hotel, and opened the doors in June 1915. The hotel flourished until the outbreak of World War II. With wartime conditions, business dramatically declined, and the hotel sat idle. Both the Navy and Air Force utilized the building off and on throughout the years for officer quarters, barracks, and as a training center. Finally, the Navy returned to build the Pacific Beach Naval Facility, which was dedicated in June 1958.

# Chapter 3

It was in May 1938 when Priscilla and Dean connected for the first time. He was tall, slim, and handsome with sparkling blue eyes. Priscilla was a freshman at Moclips High School. Dean was a junior, and the new boy in school. "When Dean showed up at school, all the girls wanted him," said Priscilla. One of her girlfriends, Llewella, who was quite popular, proclaimed she was going after him. Many girls had eyes for Dean, but Dean only had eyes for the petite vivacious pretty girl with the copper colored hair—Priscilla Dean.

Priscilla remembered the day their love story began. "When I was standing outside of Study Hall, Dean approached me, and said 'Want to go to the prom?' I couldn't wait to get back to my seat to tell Llewella that Dean had just asked me to the prom, and I had accepted."

At the time, Priscilla was dating three other fellows, but within a year, she and Dean were dating exclusively.

A twist of fate brought them together. Dean had no idea he would end up living in Pacific Beach and meet the love of his life.

* * *

Dean Messinger was born on April 20, 1920, in Grass Valley, Oregon. His mother and father had divorced when he was a baby.

His mother, Juanita, moved to California where she found work as a beautician, working for several mortuaries. Dean saw very little of his mother throughout his life.

His father, Ronnie, (Ronald) was gone much of the time looking for work, so Dean lived with his grandparents. He always said he felt it was his grandparents who raised him while they lived in Eastern Oregon.

Dean's grandparents were immigrants to Eastern Oregon where they built a ranch and raised wheat. They were prosperous until the Great Depression wreaked havoc on Americans across the nation. They lost their ranch and relocated to Pacific Beach, Washington.

Dean's father eventually remarried, and he and his new wife moved to Kelso, Washington. Dean moved with them. This new arrangement didn't work out so well for Dean. His stepmother didn't care for her stepson. She made her feelings loud and clear when he came home from high school one day in the winter of 1937, to find his belongings sitting out on the front porch. His stepmother had thrown him out. As always, Dean's father was absent most of the time due to his work, so there was no support available from his father. Dean had no choice but to leave.

What was seventeen-year-old Dean going to do with no job or a place to live? He rolled the dice, and hopped a train back to Eastern Oregon where his Uncle Parker lived. Parker was about the same age as Dean. When he connected with Parker, they decided to ride the rails together to California to look for work. Dean worked for a short time in California, but decided it wasn't for him. He was back on the rails, but this time he would go to the one place of refuge where he knew he would be welcome—his grandparents. Between riding the rails and hitchhiking, Dean ended his precipitous journey in the seaside town of Pacific Beach.

His grandparents were surprised to see their grandson on their doorstep, but they loved him dearly, and welcomed him into their home. He was happy to be living with his grandparents again. Since Dean's high school days in Kelso had been abruptly interrupted, he enrolled at Moclips High

School to finish his schooling where he would eventually meet Priscilla in the following spring of 1938.

* * *

Priscilla and Dean finished the school year together, and looked forward to the summer days. The three towns, Aloha, Pacific Beach, and Moclips, offered a plethora of activities, which helped the young people in the communities forget for a few moments about the Depression, which had been looming over their lives. They swam in the surf, played tennis, danced at Aloha Hall, or watched the latest movie release and treated themselves to ice cream afterward. There were parties to attend or a friend to visit.

Dean settled well into the community. He enjoyed his new friendships, and was thankful that fate had led him to Priscilla.

He was aware that his grandparents had been severely affected by the Depression, and he didn't want to become a burden. He found a way to pay for his keep by utilizing the beach. During the school year, he dug razor clams every morning before classes to sell to the nearby cannery. Many people dug and sold the clams. The plentiful razor clams were a saving grace for the people who lived near the beach during the Depression. The clams were not only a valuable commodity, but also provided a source of food. People didn't go hungry when they had clams to eat.

* * *

As Dean and Priscilla's love for one another grew, they spent more and more time together. They developed a ritual of walking and talking along the beach absorbing the sound of the crashing waves and breathing in the salty air of the ocean. Many a time they simply sat on the front steps of Priscilla's house where they talked, and talked, and gazed into each other's eyes. On one special night in July, they attended a dance at Pacific Beach where Dean proclaimed his love for her. From that moment on, he told Priscilla every night how much he loved her.

By the time school resumed in September 1938, Priscilla and Dean had formed an unbreakable bond. He was now a senior and she was a sophomore. They spent every free moment together, and on the evening of November 15th, Dean asked Priscilla to marry him. She said yes, but she had not yet told Dean she loved him.

Priscilla's love for Dean and his proposal for marriage was a joyous turning point during this time in her life. Unfortunately a few days later, she experienced one of the saddest times in her life.

Priscilla and Dean, around 1940

# Chapter 4

On November 20, 1938, the mill's speeder train made an unscheduled run from the Moclips timber site to Aloha. The whistle sounded, and each woman's heart skipped a beat as she watched, frozen with fear, the arrival of the speeder chugging into town. When the speeder halted, men rushed with a stretcher to carry out the latest victim from the woods. Margaret Dean stood with the other women waiting to see whom the speeder brought back. This time it was her husband, Erving Dean. He was a victim of a *widow maker*. A heavy branch had fallen on him. Frequently during storms, branches would break off and pile onto other branches. The extra weight of the fallen limbs caused the attached branch to break off, dropping from two hundred feet or more, resulting in a deadly impact on the unfortunate victim below. Erving was still alive, and an ambulance rushed him to a hospital in Hoquiam. He was sent home, but died a short time later of a heart attack. He and Margaret had been married twenty-eight years.

Priscilla wrote in her diary,

*November 21, 1938*

*Dear God, Daddy died last night.*

*November 22, 1938*

*God, please make it easier for Mom to bear. Thank you, dear Lord, that it was so easy – the way he wanted it.*

*November 25, 1938*

*Daddy's funeral was today. Beautiful flowers and sermon. Mrs. Rowe sang. Lots of people were there. God rest his soul to heaven.*

The night of the funeral, Priscilla told Dean she loved him.

Priscilla's mother was now a widow, and she had no choice but to square her shoulders and take control of her and Priscilla's life. She had always known the day could come when her husband might fall victim to the woods. With no insurance or savings left behind, she had to find another way to earn an income, and an inexpensive place to live. It wouldn't be easy with the hard times of the Depression still lingering. Margaret and Priscilla moved out of their Aloha house.

With admiration, Priscilla said, "My mother grieved, but she was a very dependable, staunch woman. She took good care of me."

# Chapter 5

The year 1939 brought many changes.

Margaret found a temporary job and a place for her and Priscilla to stay at the hotel in Aloha. Priscilla helped her mother as much as she could after school.

Dean graduated from Moclips High School in May, and went to work for the Aloha sawmill. By August, he switched to working in the woods. Priscilla, of course, wasn't happy about his decision, with her father's death still so fresh in her mind.

School resumed on September 5th.. Priscilla returned as a senior, and turned seventeen on September 14th. During her last year of school, Priscilla lived alone in a small beach cabin at Pacific Beach. "It was more like a shack," commented Priscilla. Her mother had found work in Aberdeen as a cook, but didn't want to uproot Priscilla from her high school class in her final year.

Priscilla and Dean continued to discuss marriage, and planned to marry soon after she graduated.

The country was beginning to recover from ten years of the Great Depression. The Wall Street Crash of 1920 had come after a decade of a burgeoning economy shortly after the Great War ended. Americans looked forward to prosperous times again.

The New York World's Fair had opened on April 30th, with the grand theme—*Building the World of Tomorrow.* It was a beacon of light, and was advertised as the fair for everyone.

President Roosevelt gave the opening speech. The fair covered 1,216 acres in Flushing Meadows, New York. Over two hundred thousand people attended. The fair ran for a year and a half, and closed on October 27, 1940.

Just when life looked promising, Americans began to hear rumblings about war in Europe. Then on September 1, 1939, without warning, Adolph Hitler and Nazi Germany invaded Poland. Now Britain and France were at war with Germany. Americans continued to hear news about the besiege of Europe by Nazi Germany and Fascist Italy. The words, *Second World War,* seeped into everyday life, but involvement felt distant since the only way they heard any news was on the radio or in the newspaper.

Priscilla noted in her diary in September that she was tired of always hearing comments about the war in Europe and Adolph Hitler. Even the youth were aware of the uncertain times.

The United States tried to remain neutral and avoid the conflict. On September 5th, the United States declared neutrality and Congress passed the Neutrality Act. But after Nazi Germany seized Poland, President Roosevelt promised financial assistance and supplies in support of the Allies in Europe. No American troop support would be sent, however. Americans wanted to believe him.

# Chapter 6

The summer of 1940 was the beginning of a new chapter in Priscilla's life. She was now a graduate of Moclips High School, and her mother landed a job at the celebrated Kelly's Dude Ranch in Queets, Washington, as a cook and housekeeper. The ranch owners hired Priscilla to assist her mother and to perform various other tasks. The commute to Queets from Pacific Beach was slightly over an hour's drive.

In the 1920s, Malcolm Kelly settled in the Queets River Valley, and built a cattle ranch. It occurred to him his ranch could accommodate guests to enjoy an *Old West* style of living and bask in the beauty and grandeur of the Olympic Peninsula. The ranch offered camping, horseback riding, fishing, nature walks and hiking; and when in season, picking wild blackberries or huckleberries. There was croquet, horseshoes, and singing and telling stories around evening campfires. For those who wanted to see more of the wondrous Peninsula, Mr. Kelly guided guests on packhorse trips into the mountains. If they wanted a more adventurous experience, they could take a canoe trip down the Queets River to the Pacific Ocean.

On June 19th, seventeen-year-old Priscilla arrived at Queets. She wrote in her diary, *Well, here I am at Kelly's. Am kinda scared too! Hope I make it okay.*

The next morning, Priscilla was up at 7:00 a.m. By the end of the day she was acquainted with everything and everyone, and finished the chores. It was hard work, but she liked it.

Every evening she played a game of Chinese Checkers with Mr. Kelly.

Priscilla helped in the kitchen, waited tables for the guests, and was thrilled when she received a tip. She ironed, laundered sheets, made up the guest beds, and cleaned all the cabins.

Priscilla wrote in her diary on July 19th, *Washed fifty-four sheets today. Hot weather.* After she laundered the sheets in the wringer washing machine, she hung all fifty-four sheets on the clothesline to dry in the sun.

She picked cherries, raspberries and blackberries, helped harvest the garden for Mrs. Kelly's home-cooked meals, and helped the men with the haying. On the Fourth of July she helped serve a picnic on the lawn under the trees for several guests. They drank pink lemonade.

Mr. Kelly advertised his ranch as a guest ranch in the Olympics. It provided sleeping quarters for thirty-eight guests in the ranch house and nearby cabins. The ranch was self-sufficient with its own water and lighting, and fitted out with indoor plumbing and showers. The home-cooked meals were served family style. The Kelly gardens offered a variety of fresh vegetables, and they had their own poultry, eggs, rabbits, beef, fresh milk, butter, and dairy foods. There was even a small store, which carried such items as fishing tackle, tobacco, and drugs. Rates were $6.00 a day for single, or $10.00 for double. The week rate was $36.00 for single, and $60.00 for double. Saddle horses were $5.00 a day, pack horses, $4.50 a day, and guides $10.00 a day.

Although Priscilla worked hard, she enjoyed some of the amenities in her free time. She took walks, target-practiced, went horseback riding, and spent time at the Queets River. The only thing missing was Dean. She missed him, and watched for his letters in the mail daily. One day he surprised her, and showed up at the ranch.

On July 19th, Priscilla was excited to receive her first paycheck for the month in the amount of $19.15, plus she had earned tips from the guests. The ranch was busy with guests the entire summer including Labor Day in September.

One day in August, Priscilla's mother, Margaret, who had left the ranch for some time, came back. Mother and daughter had an opportunity for a nice long talk. Priscilla hadn't told Margaret about her and Dean's plans to get married that year. When Priscilla told her mother, she was relieved to learn of her mother's approval. Priscilla wrote Dean that night with the good news. The wedding was on.

* * *

It was October 26, 1940. Priscilla and Dean stood in the First Christian Church in Aberdeen, Washington, and exchanged their wedding vows. Priscilla became Mrs. Ronald Dean Messinger. She looked beautiful in her full-length ivory satin gown accented with lace, and the crowning touch of a headpiece and waltz length tulle veil edged in lace. She carried a bouquet of creamy-white spider chrysanthemums and deep pink roses. Her handsome groom wore a black double-breasted suit and striped tie with a single deep pink rosebud boutonniere pinned on his left lapel.

The newlyweds honeymooned in a plush hotel in Aberdeen. Presently in 2017, Priscilla still has the napkin from the hotel dining room, which she saved in a scrapbook, along with her wedding dress safely stored in her cedar chest.

They settled in a modest cedar clad cottage surrounded with a weathered picket fence at Pacific Beach. The constant roar of the ocean surf often lured them to the sandy beach, which was just a short walk away. Strolling along the beach was still their favorite pastime.

Dean continued to work at the mill. He had been working there since his graduation from high school. Because Dean was young and inexperienced, he was hired as a whistle punk. His job was to send signals from a remote work site to the donkey puncher by jerking the whistle wire in long or short blasts to alert the puncher when the timber was ready to be moved.

Priscilla felt uneasy whenever Dean headed off to the forest. "I told him he had to get a job away from the woods." She had already lost her father from working in the woods, and feared Dean would be injured or killed too.

Her fears were well founded. One day, after Dean had been at work for several hours, a truck pulled up in front of their house. A man stepped out holding Dean's boots, covered in blood, and set them on her doorstep. He told her Dean had been injured and taken to the hospital. Memories of her father's accident flooded her mind. She prayed Dean was all right. She rushed to the hospital and found him. An axe had gashed his leg. Priscilla begged him to get a job away from the woods. He promised he would.

Dean knew to keep his promise to Priscilla, they would have to move to an area that didn't revolve solely around the logging industry. The couple moved south and further inland to the Longview-Kelso area, where Dean found employment at Hart Construction Company. The company specialized in heavy construction bridgework. Kelso was a logical choice for Dean since he had lived there with his father, and his father was still there.

Priscilla and Dean enjoyed their life together. They worked hard to forge their future, but with the atmosphere of war in Europe, there was uncertainty. They could feel the tension, and feared that sooner or later, the United States would be compelled to enter the war.

Priscilla and Dean married October 26, 1940

# Chapter 7

It was Sunday, December 7, 1941. While Americans went about their daily rituals, startling news exploded over the airwaves. Without warning, Japan attacked Pearl Harbor causing massive destruction and casualties. Priscilla and Dean, along with Americans across the nation, were in a state of shock and disbelief. They hovered over the radio to hear every detail.

The next day, President Roosevelt spoke to Americans and made the chilling announcement about the surprise attack on Pearl Harbor, calling December 7th a date that would *live in infamy*, and the United States was declaring war on Japan. The couple had barely begun their life together, and now their future was uncertain. It would be only a matter of time before Dean may be called, especially since they didn't have children.

* * *

The people on the West Coast felt vulnerable. Hawaii had been attacked without warning. Would the Japanese land on their shores next? The United States military considered the threat a possibility, and immediately stationed troops onto the beaches. By afternoon of the announcement, trucks filled with soldiers rolled into the quiet town of Pacific Beach. They were ordered to establish beach patrols and set up gun emplacements.

With so many soldiers coming into town without warning, there were very few places available for the soldiers to sleep. The soldiers took their sleeping bags anywhere they could roll them out—private homes, motels, or any place they could find. The Army discovered a skating rink owned and operated by the Pacific Beach Ladies Aid. The rink became the Army headquarters and mess hall.

A blackout status was ordered for anyone living along the coast so there wouldn't be any visible light out to sea. At night, people covered their windows with blackout curtains. Streetlights were turned off. When they drove their vehicles, they were required to use their fog lights rather than bright headlights. Unfortunately, these driving conditions caused some accidents both for drivers and pedestrians.

Many of the people living in beach shacks volunteered to take turns to watch the ocean horizon for any evidence of Japanese submarines lurking along the coastline.

The community was cooperative and supportive. Their men were already off to war, and since most of them had worked at the mill, the women took their place at the mill.

Like many other towns across the nation, the townspeople set up a *canteen* for the soldiers. It was set up in a small building nicknamed *THE HUT*. The local cooks rallied, and supplied the canteen with cakes, cookies and other delicacies. A jukebox was donated, and the girls in town were very happy to donate their time to entertain the young soldiers.

The community of Pacific Beach, which had been Dean and Priscilla's former playground along with thousands of tourists, changed dramatically. In 1942, the popular Pacific Beach Honeymoon Hotel became a casualty of the war. The war had caused a drastic decline in business due to restrictions on gas and travel.

The Navy recognized the stagnant facility, situated up on the bluff, as a prime property to buy for an important use. It established an anti-aircraft training center along with gun installations set up on the beach; and the hotel, which formerly housed tourists, was converted into barracks. The guest cottages became officers' quarters. The beach site was ideal to fire guns over the ocean at targets towed by planes while not putting the public in danger. Civilian vessels weren't allowed in the area twenty-four hours a day. Instead of hearing the sound of the pounding surf, nearby residents heard the thunder of the 16mm guns. The whole town shook. The residents got tired of crooked pictures on their walls, and finally removed them.

The military activity in town lasted until the end of the war. For four years the community watched three hundred soldiers train every morning, and watched airplanes overhead towing orange nylon sleeves. Many of the townspeople collected the sleeves that broke loose, and used them in creative ways. One resident ended up with a pair of bright orange pajamas.

* * *

The nation changed in many ways. Japanese-Americans became victims of the war in their own country. Before the Pearl Harbor attack, through hard work and family unity, they became successful entrepreneurs and business owners. Many were farmers, hotel owners and managers. The immigrant generation known as *Issei* were vigilant to make sure their children, the second generation, *Nisei,* received an education.

The government was suspicious that a West Coast espionage network had been formed, and Japanese-Americans were the prime suspects. Officials began arresting leading Japanese and Japanese-American citizens. No evidence was found, but despite the finding, President Roosevelt signed Executive Order 9066, on February 19, 1942. The Order authorized the removal and transfer of approximately 110,000 Japanese and Japanese-Americans living on the West Coast. They were moved to ten inland internment camps, and forced to live in tarpaper huts enclosed with barbed wire and guard towers.

Many of the second-generation Japanese-Americans

proved their loyalty by joining the fight. They enlisted in the 442nd Regimental Combat Team, which was established in early 1943. It was the first combat unit in U.S. history to be comprised exclusively of second generation *Nisei* Japanese-Americans. They fought valiantly and brought honor to their families.

Beginning in September 1943, the 442nd's 100th Battalion fought in the European Theater for nine months. During a bloody forty-day battle in Monte Cassino in early 1944, the unit fought courageously and endured high casualties. After this battle, the battalion became known as the *Purple Heart Battalion*.

Later in 1944, the unit lost more men during the rescue of the 1st Battalion of the 141st U.S. Infantry Regiment, known as the *Texas Lost Battalion,* which had been trapped behind enemy lines, earning the Japanese battalion a Presidential Unit Citation. The *Nisei* battalion became the most decorated combat unit of its size in Army history. Out of 14,000 men, 9,486 were awarded Purple Hearts.

* * *

Despite the war, Priscilla and Dean continued to live their life as normal as possible, but they always kept an ear tuned in to the news. They brought in the New Year, 1942, together, and wondered what it would bring. By spring, the government established rationing programs. Priscilla and Dean, along with families across the nation, were issued ration stamps, which provided them with an allotment to purchase such food items as meat, sugar, butter, vegetables and fruit. The people living in the Pacific Beach area were fortunate to supplement their food supply with the bounties from the sea. They dug razor clams, picked up oysters, and fished in the surf. Gas, tires and clothing were also rationed. It was patriotic for women not to wear hosiery.

Many Americans responded by growing Victory Gardens for more food just as their predecessors had done during

World War I. Drivers were initiated for collecting scrap metal, aluminum cans, and rubber to be recycled for producing the much needed armaments. They sold war bonds to help raise money for the war.

Priscilla had good news for Dean that summer—she was pregnant. Since Dean was making a stable income, they felt financially comfortable and were thrilled about the baby. The baby was due in February of the following year, 1943.

February was an eventful month for the Messingers. First, Dean had accepted a job at Hart Construction Company. Then, Priscilla went into labor, and they rushed to the Cowlitz General Hospital where she gave birth to a baby girl. They named their daughter Carol Ann.

The family of three would only have five and a half months together before Dean would leave to train as a member of the newly formed United States Naval Construction Battalion.

By summertime, Dean had been accepted into to the Seabees. When they learned he was entering the Naval Seabee program, Priscilla and Dean had only a few days left to spend together. Priscilla dreaded the day when she would be sending him off from the train station.

Dean, baby (Carol Ann), and Priscilla. Picture taken on the day Dean shipped out, 1943

# Chapter 8

Dean was on a train heading to Norfolk, Virginia. It had only been a couple of days since they parted at the train station, and Priscilla already missed him, and wondered when she would receive his first letter. She didn't have to wait long. The mailman brought the first letter from Dean postmarked August 5, 1943, mailed from Boise, Idaho, enroute to his destination. He'd kept his promise to write to her on his first opportunity. She quickly opened the envelope, and read the coveted letter.

*Dearest Darling & Baby…How is the baby? Fine I hope….*
*Well, honey, I haven't much to say so will close for now. Will write again before I get back there, and a nice long letter as soon as I arrive.*
*All my love to you both,*
*Dean.*

Priscilla held the letter close to her heart and read it over and over. She marked the envelope, *First Letter.*

A few days later, she received another letter from Dean, postmarked August 7th. He was now in Chicago, Illinois, housed for an eight-hour layover at the Chicago Servicemen's Center.

*Dearest Wife & Baby…I wish I could leave you an address so you could write, but I won't be able to do that until I get to Norfolk.*

*I always made fun of the U.S.O., but I will take it all back. It is a wonderful institution....*

*There was never anything so welcome as the hot shower I got here and the place to shave.*

*We have talked to lots of sailors on the trip, no Sea Bees. But they all tell us we are in for a tough old grind. I guess all Sea Bees are given commando training by the Marines and from what they say they're plenty hard. But then three weeks of it won't be so hard. I think that I am just as tough as they* are...

*With all my love to you both.*

*Dean.*

Priscilla laid his letter next to the first one, and marked the envelope, *Second Letter.*

Another letter arrived postmarked August 11th. Dean had arrived at the induction center in Virginia where he would stay for three days. He received a physical, despite having gone through a physical earlier. This was where his wavy hair was cut short, and his clothes were issued. Boot camp was next. On to Camp Perry, in Williamsburg. Boot camp would last for four weeks and he would be sent to Rhode Island for advanced training.

The next letter, postmarked, August 13th, came from Camp Perry. Finally, an address where Priscilla could write to her husband. He was anxious for her letters. Dean wrote to Priscilla almost daily. He described the living conditions—it was hot and he missed all the green trees in Washington state. Three men had dropped from the heat during one of the drills, and one got sunstroke. Dean wrote in detail about the training and strict drills, and how friends were split up. He finally found his friend, Jack, who was located two barracks away from him.

Dean learned that Priscilla would receive $87.00 a month from the Navy. He told her he was required to sign up for $10,000 worth of insurance which would cost him $6.60 a month leaving him with $18.00 a month on his end. He worried how she was coping. In his letter, he asked,

*How has the car been behaving? All right I hope. Have you got a job yet?*

In every letter, Dean poured his heart out to Priscilla about how he missed her and the baby, and how much he loved them. Sometimes he didn't have a lot to tell her, or couldn't divulge details about what he was doing, but his love and longing for her and the baby were constant.

Dean in uniform, 1943, Dean's hat (still in safe keeping)

# Chapter 9

Priscilla worked as a waitress at a local cafe in Kelso, but even with tips, there wouldn't be enough money to cover their bills. Then she heard about the pleas from the United States government asking women to fill the shoes of the men who went off to war.

After December 7th, the United States became involved in a two-theater war, Europe and the South Pacific. When millions of men went to war, they left behind a large void in the labor work force. Not only was there a demand for manpower, but there was also a demand for equipment to fight the war. Priscilla needed a dependable job, and Uncle Sam needed her.

There were many jobs to fill. Women learned to pump gas and to drive taxicabs, trucks and buses. Two of the largest industries in the Northwest where thousands of women applied for work were Boeing aircraft plants with branches in Seattle and Renton, and the Kaiser shipyard located on the Columbia and Willamette Rivers in Portland and Vancouver. Boeing produced thousands of the B-17 *Flying Fortress* and the advanced bomber, the B-29 *Superfortress*. The Kaiser plants constructed oil tankers, *baby flattop* aircraft carriers and merchant *Liberty* ships. By 1943, there was also a top-secret guarded facility, which produced plutonium for the world's first atom bomb, at Hanford in Eastern Washington.

There was a help wanted ad by Boeing:

*WOMEN! Even if you've never done anything except housework, there's almost certainly a job for you here at Boeing – a clean and pleasant one – and you can take pride in being a Boeing worker. Your husband – your son – your brother or boyfriend will be proud that you are doing your part in building the axis-blasting Flying Fortress.*

When Priscilla learned about the Boeing plant that had opened in June 1943, in Aberdeen, and heard it paid good wages, she knew it was her opportunity to gain a better paying job, and to serve her country. While her husband built, defended and fought overseas, she would be helping to build the equipment in the factory to help win the war. Boeing needed to open more plants to meet its production goal, and the Aberdeen plant became one of ten branch assembly plants established in western Washington. These plants brought a welcome increase in jobs after so much unemployment in the recent Depression years.

Across the nation, thousands of Americans from all walks of life answered the call for help and joined the work force. People of different nationalities and ages stepped up. There were housewives, socialites, professors and teachers, actresses, musicians, bank clerks, lawyers, or like Priscilla, waitresses. The motto, *We Can Do It* became the theme. Some women joined the WAVES and the WACS, and others volunteered at the USO facilities. The more women at work, the sooner the war would be won. *Life* magazine referred to female war workers as the *Glamour Girls of 1942.*

Priscilla made a difficult decision. She lived in Kelso, and now she needed to move to Aberdeen, and find an apartment to work at the Boeing plant. It would be impossible to take her baby with her. She asked her brother, Myron, and his wife, Merie, as well as other extended family members, if Carol Ann could stay with them until the end of the war. The family members agreed to help her. Priscilla saw very little of her daughter during that time. Carol Ann became an unwitting participant in her own sacrifice for the war by not being raised by her mother and father for over two years.

Priscilla reflected back to the day she stood in the Boeing office, "I can still picture the man, seventy-four years ago, filling out my application. When he asked me my name, I replied 'Priscilla Dean Messinger'. He said my name was too long for my badge. He looked at me, and told me my hair reminded him of a copper penny. He said my name was going to be Penny. From then on, I've always been called Penny." But to her husband, Dean, she was always Priscilla.

She was photographed, finger printed, and recorded as a home front worker. Boeing would train her for a specialty such as a welder, electrician, or riveter—all roles previously held by men only. Like her mother before her, Penny took over a man's job during wartime. She joined the ranks as one of many *Rosie the Riveters* at the Boeing Factory.

Each worker received *The Girl Mechanic's Manual,* which emphasized safety around the heavy equipment. They were instructed on how to come to work. It was important to wear the correct apparel to the job. Loose flowing sleeves could get caught in moving machinery and cause severe injury. They needed to wear tight or short sleeves for safety. The same was true for hair, loose flowing hair was dangerous and could also get caught in machinery. Also, hair in the face could prevent seeing their work properly, which could cause an accident. Wearing a bandana or hair net was recommended. They learned that the machines had many parts, which could catch on rings, watches, chains and other adornments. They said, "Leave your jewelry at home." Long fingernails were taboo as well as high heels. Heels could catch easily causing the wearer to trip and fall or even break an ankle. The women should wear comfortable shoes with wide low heels. In some jobs such as welding or where there might be flying particles, they needed to be sure to protect their eyes with shields and eye goggles. Without due care, they could lose their eyesight.

Boeing worked with a major department store in Seattle to

provide a working fashion for the women. Penny wore one of the designs--canvas coveralls styled as a white one-piece, short-sleeved jumpsuit, which included her name in red embroidery on the front, and the word *Superfortress* embroidered in red across the back. She wore her hair up, and covered with a bandana. Penny kept her uniform in her cedar chest through the years, and it still fits her.

She was proud to be a part of the work force fighting to win the war. "I worked on the B-17 Flying Fortress, and the B-29 Superfortress. The B-29 was the plane that dropped the atomic bomb," she said.

With the fear of an attack on the West Coast by the Japanese, precautions were taken. Boeing disguised the plants by creating a camouflaged scene on the rooftops. In Seattle, an entire fake fool-the-eye neighborhood was put in place on the Boeing plant rooftops. At the Aberdeen plant, vegetation camouflage was installed on the rooftop.

The Aberdeen employees were proud to participate in an important top-secret project on the B-17E Flying Fortress called the *Stinger of Death.* The older Fortresses, the B-17C and D, had an *Achilles heel* – there wasn't adequate gun protection to protect the tail section of the plane. The Japanese fighters recognized this weakness, and swooped down toward a Fortress's tail section, and attacked, crippling many of the Fortresses. This weakness was short-lived, however. Boeing went into swift action and manufactured the B-17E equipping it with twin machine guns in the tail, calling it the stinger turret.

When the new Fortresses flew into battle, the Nippon flyers expected a soft target, but instead flew into a stream of 50-caliber machine bullets. The Fortress became known as the best combat plane to have ever been built.

In July 1944, the Aberdeen branch along with other Boeing aircraft branches in Western Washington received the Army-Navy Production Award, which was the highest award that could be given to a war production firm. The award was presented in the form of a pennant to be flown over the branch plant. Each employee, including Penny, received an E-pin at a special ceremony. The letter *E* represented excellency in production. At the age of ninety-five, Penny still has her pin.

As described by the Undersecretary of War, Robert P. Patterson:

"This award is your nation's tribute to your spirit of patriotism and your production effort...This symbol is accorded only to those plants which are exceeding all production expectations in view of the facilities at their command."

During the presentation, Patterson said, "I have full confidence that your present high achievement is indicative of what you will do in the future."

Penny was one of six million American women who worked in the home-front factories during World War II. The motto *Women at Work* appeared on posters and pamphlets everywhere. Wives, mothers, and sweethearts did their part to help win the war by filling the jobs left vacant by the men who went off to fight. As these production soldiers punched in every day for work in the factories, shipyards and munitions plants, they proved they could perform a man's job, and do it well.

*Rosie the Riveter* became a national symbol for American women on the home front doing vital work to help win the war.

A pilot had even named his B-17 *Rosie's Riveters.* When he flew his plane to perform daylight bombing raids over Germany, the symbol could be seen proudly displayed on the nose of the plane.

In 1942, Redd Evans and John Jacob Loeb wrote the song, "Rosie the Riveter".

There were *Rosie the Riveter* posters everywhere. One

famous poster became the cover of the *Saturday Evening Post* featuring the well-known Norman Rockwell painting, *Rosie*, of a confident, tough, hard working woman holding a rivet gun.

As a result of World War II, another symbol of female strength was born. It came in the form of the comic book character, *Wonder Woman*. It was created in 1941 by a male DC Comics consultant and psychologist, and the *Ladies' Home Journal* columnist, Dr. William Moulton Marston.

*Wonder Woman's* life began as a princess of an all-female island. Her life changed when she rescued and nursed a pilot who had been shot down near her island. She fell in love with him, and followed him to America, where she would help fight against threats to America by the Axis nations. She would fight bravely against Nazism and Fascism, resulting in *Wonder Woman* becoming the first female inducted into the DC Comics superhero's League of Justice. Later, in the early 1970s, *Wonder Woman* reappeared on the cover of *Ms. Magazine* introduced by the editor, Gloria Steinem. For the women working on the home front during World War II, *Wonder Woman* paralleled their own discoveries of untapped skills and unrecognized power. Their lives were forever changed.

* * *

After the war, the soldiers returned and reclaimed their jobs. The women were expected to leave and resume their roles before the war, but many women didn't want to give up the freedom and independence they had gained. They were now confident to take care of themselves, and earning their own money was liberating. When husbands returned home to their wives after the war, they found different women waiting for them. Many women decided to keep working, and found new jobs if they weren't offered continued employment where they had worked.

Priscilla (Penny) and friend with tool kits in hand ready for work at the Boeing factory, 1943

Priscilla (Penny) as a riveter at Boeing, 1943

Priscilla, an independent woman, 1943

Priscilla modeling her uniform, present day 2017

# Chapter 10

Penny and Dean continued to write each other every day. The mail became their lifeline. Despite writing daily, sometimes a letter wouldn't arrive for several days, and when it did, several letters might arrive. Dean continued to describe his training, but most of all, he told Priscilla how much he missed her and the baby.

Finally, in his letter dated September 10, 1943, from Camp Endicott, Davisville, Rhode Island, Dean was ecstatic to tell Penny he was granted a ten-day leave to come home in October.

On September 16th, Dean wrote to Penny and told her he had drawn his school, which was Wharves and Docks.

*Just what I wanted. They have three pile drivers here in Narragansett Bay. We drive piling and build docks one day, and go to school the next.*

He continued, *I am sure lucky – no KP duty, work detail, nor fire watch. Don't even have to clean up my bunk and locker. Have an apprentice to do that. Don't have to stand in chow lines either, we just go earlier than the rest. There are about eighty of us out of the seventeen hundred they picked to do the different trade schools. The rest have to drill and do the work.*

In a letter dated September 21st, Dean described rifle training. *We will go to the range for five days. We'll shoot for marksmanship, and have forty shots with a possible score of 200. A score of 135 is a marksman, 160 is sharp shooter, and 175 is expert. I want that experts medal.*

Dean wrote in his September 27th letter, *We'll be at a camp in Sun Valley for a week, which has the same conditions as Island X. Chow halls are outside and you have to stand to eat. Outside cans and everything!*

He told her the next training would be with the Thompson machine guns for seven days. They'd be staying in Quonset huts at the range with twelve men to a hut. Oil stoves would be used for heat since the temperature at night was cold.

On October 9, 1943, Dean received his Certificate of Completion for completing the advanced course in Wharves & Docks, N.C.T.C., Camp Endicott, Rhode Island.

Dean relayed disappointing news in his October 15th letter to Penny. Instead of being transferred to the West Coast as he had hoped, he was being sent to Mississippi. Part of his leave time would be used up on the travel time so they would only have three or four days together. His leave was scheduled to begin on the 25th. He noted that Congress made it law that the men must get leave before shipping out.

On October 20th, Penny received a telegram. It unnerved her since she wasn't expecting one. It read, "Send all money can spare. Leave starts twenty-fifth."

Because Dean wasn't flying from the West Coast as anticipated, he was short on money for the more expensive fare. Penny immediately responded, and wired $75.00 to him.

* * *

Together again, but not long enough. Penny and Dean couldn't get enough of each other. Carol Ann was now nearly three months older. It was disappointing for Dean to miss out on three months of their baby's life, but soon he would be missing many more months of her life. Before long, he would be separated from his beloved wife and child for an undetermined length of time. He knew he was shipping out some time after the New Year to Island X, and this was his last leave. Their time together flew by, and they had to say goodbye again at the train station.

Penny was alone again, and waited for Dean's first letter. She received his letter, dated November 10th.

*Dearest Darling,*

*I suppose you wonder why you haven't got a card from me. Well, dear, I wanted to, and intended to, but I never got off the train till I got to Chicago….*

*Honey, I sure hated to leave you the way I did at the station, but I couldn't have stayed there any longer or I would have broken down. Darling, that was the hardest thing I have ever had to do….*

*All my Love,*

*Dean.*

*P.S. Please write long letters, honey.*

# Chapter 11

In early February 1944, the Seabees of the 130th Naval Construction Battalion boarded a troop ship destined for Island X. Dean had no idea where he was going except to some island in the Pacific.

During the first week, Penny received a Notice of Change of Address from the United States Navy Department. All mail from that point on would come and go through the Fleet Post Office in San Francisco, and would be censored. She knew the day had come—Dean was being shipped out.

After Dean shipped out, Penny received her first letter from him dated February 8, 1944, with the notation, *Somewhere in the Pacific*. The Seabees had disembarked onto the island of Oahu, the United States Territory of Hawaii. They received strict orders not to reveal their locale for fear the enemy might intercept a letter giving away their position.

The Seabees would become directly involved in the Pacific Theater of Operations. These men would earn the respect and gratitude of the Allied fighting men who either served with them or followed them in their path. Eighty percent of the Naval Construction Battalions concentrated on the three Pacific roads—the North, Central, and South to Southwest areas. With their extensive training, creativity, and fortitude, they built and fought their way toward victory.

While Penny was helping to build airplanes back home to help win the war, Dean was building and fighting overseas. As months went by, the Seabees moved from island to island swooping into the war zone to build advance bases. Sometimes they went in before the Marines, and other times with the Marines. The Seabees built roads and bridges, set up communications, barracks, mess halls, warehouses, and repair shops. When the Marines captured an enemy airstrip on an island, the Seabees went to work repairing the damage caused by the battle. Many times the Japanese zeroed in on them as they worked. They stopped only long enough to defend themselves and what they built.

* * *

In the early morning hours of June 15, 1944, on Landing Ship Tank #40 (LST), which was the length of a football field, Dean and his Seabee comrades (302 NCB) and a division of Marines (2nd Bn., 8th Reg., 2nd Div.), awoke to the call for muster. It was the signal for the anticipated landing and battle on the beaches of the Japanese island of Saipan. No one had slept well, if not at all, waiting for this day. Breakfast was served on the mess deck. No one spoke. Their minds were focused on the upcoming battle. It was D-Day. They double-checked their backpacks making sure important necessities hadn't been forgotten, and re-inspected their rifles while picking up an extra supply of ammunition.

Then the Admiral in charge gave the order, "Land the landing force." Thirty-four LSTs lined up. The huge doors opened on the bows of the ships, and the ramps dropped into the water. The men poured out.

Next came the AMTRAKs, loaded with Marines ready for the fight. The AMTRAKs were assault amphibian tractors to carry troops and special amphibian tanks. Each one was equipped with a 75mm howitzer canon and a heavy machine gun, which was capable of taking out Japanese bunkers and pillboxes.

Four pontoon barges (22 x 40 feet) were chained to the top deck on Dean's LST. They were to be used to haul ammunition. Some of the other LSTs carried long pontoon sections strapped to the sides, which would become a floating pier to allow the landing craft to unload. This was one of Dean's specialties.

The Marines' mission was to take and hold the beachhead. Before the Marines moved onto the beach, twenty-four light gunboats swept the beach firing 4.5-inch rockets and 40mm canons. Additionally, seven fighter planes strafed the beach, and twelve bombers hit the area with twelve hundred pound bombs. All this activity didn't stop the Japanese who were dug in, but their communication links to their commanders were destroyed. The amphibian tanks were the first wave, and began firing heavy weapons as they moved toward the beach. The AMTRACKs carrying the troops followed. The troops received extra assistance from the two battleships, the *California* and *Tennessee*. Both these ships had been hit at Pearl Harbor and lost sailors. Now they were shooting back.

The Seabees' job was to get food and ammunition onto the beach, but they had to remain on the LSTs until the enemy fire ceased. The Marines were outnumbered, but with good leadership, weaponry, courage and fortitude, they took the beach. That night, Dean and his fellow Seabees were ordered to use the cover of darkness to launch the causeway floating piers from the LSTs. Once the causeways were in the water, the crews took them through the narrow channel to the Charan Kanoa beachhead. By daybreak, the pier was operational, and they were unloading the much-needed supplies from the landing craft.

The next day they were ordered to launch all the barges carried on seven of the LSTs. Before they completed their task, they fell under enemy gunfire. Fortunately, the enemy missed. The LST moved and the launching continued.

Once the barges were in the ocean, the Seabees boarded the barges and steered them along the side transports to retrieve nets full of ammunition and C-Rations.

As their barge moved toward the beach, the Seabees saw firsthand the horror of war. Dean saw an AMTRAK turned upside down that had taken a direct hit. They saw several other damaged AMTRAKs and amphibian tanks spread around the beach area. They saw dead Marines floating in the water, and dead Japanese soldiers covered the beachhead. Defense took precedence over burial detail. It was the scene of a bloody battle.

Armed with their rifles, Dean and some of the other Seabees took a walk to the Charan Kanoa village. When they arrived, they saw houses and buildings destroyed, but didn't see any evidence of the dead. Then they came upon a baseball diamond where at the home base plate, they discovered a machine gun and three dead Japanese soldiers. As they walked further toward the outside of the village, they found several bodies, torn to pieces. Evidence of recent counterattacks.

On June 19th, units of the U.S. Army's 27th Infantry Division landed and advanced to take the Aslito airfield. The Japanese leader, Saito, could not hold the airfield and was forced to abandon it.

* * *

The Seabees continued their job of moving ammunition and supplies to the beach for fifty-four days exposed to the weather—sometimes blazing sun and sometimes pouring rain. They ate C-Rations and slept on the barges. Sleeping next to ammunition wasn't the most comforting feeling. The enemy was still holed up on the island, and shooting at the ammunition was a possibility. One day the Japanese did shoot, and hit the ammo dump. Dean and the other men weren't injured, but any of them who were close to the explosion, lost some of their hearing. Dean lost at least fifty percent of his hearing in his right ear, and had trouble hearing for years to come.

The Americans were successful in cutting off the Imperial Japanese Army from access to supplies, and continued to push back. The commander, Saito, moved his troops to the defensible Mt. Tapotchau. The mountain was nicknamed *Hell's Pocket, Purple Ridge,* and *Death Valley.* The Japanese hid during daylight in the many caves of the volcanic mountainous terrain, and attacked during the night. The Americans cleared the caves with the use of flamethrower teams and machine guns.

The battle of Saipan was near the end, but Saito was defiant, and with nowhere left to retreat, planned a final suicidal *banzai* charge. In the half-light of dawn on July 7, 1944, Saito launched the largest *banzai* attack of the entire war. A bugle sounded, and approximately 4,000 Japanese soldiers, armed with rifles and spears, shouting "Banzai!" charged the American front lines. For the first time during the war, the Army and Marines would fight side by side. The Americans on the front lines were outnumbered three to one. The attackers broke through the lines of both the Marine and Army units. The 105th Infantry took the brunt with 650 killed and wounded. They fired their rifles until they ran out of ammo, and used their machine guns until the barrels overheated. It was a killing field.

A surviving infantryman said,

"There were so damn many Japs you couldn't kill them all before they had overrun our advance positions and penetrated rearward."

The Americans set up a second perimeter along the beach fighting with their backs to the ocean, but the fierce resistance of both the Army and Marine units prevailed.

After the fifteen-hour long battle was over, 4,300 Japanese soldiers and civilians lay dead. Bodies fell so fast that the American gunners had to maneuver around them to continue firing. It was a gruesome sight of carnage.

After three weeks of battle on Saipan, there were more than 3,000 U.S. deaths and over 13,000 wounded. Nearly all of the 30,000 Japanese troops died. Over 22,000 Japanese civilians died which included the civilians who committed suicide. The Japanese propaganda had convinced the civilians that being under control of the American occupation would be their worst fate. Thousands of Japanese civilians jumped to their death into the ocean from the high cliffs on the northern end of the island. Saito, along with the other commanders with him, committed suicide in one of the caves.

* * *

Penny didn't receive as many letters during this time, but she kept every newspaper clipping related to Dean's battalion in the Pacific islands. One clipping was from the Aberdeen Daily World, dated July 11, 1944, which described the Saipan battle.

*Bloody Friday - Saipan*

*Throughout the night machine guns rattled and rifles had rattled, and when the Japanese hit at dawn, U.S. Forces started firing.*

*Americans and Japanese threw grenades at each other from thirty feet, swapped rifle fire at ten feet, lunged at each other with bayonets at arms' length.*

The Seabees had stayed with the barges, and when they gazed at the sky in the early morning light, they saw star shells bursting over the distant battlefield, and heard the rumble of artillery. Later that morning, they received news about a serious enemy attack that had been thwarted. Soon, the wounded carried on stretchers filled the pier to be transported to the hospital ships.

On July 9th, the island was declared secure. Seizing the island became one of the most strategic moments during the war. The soldiers and the Seabees were ordered to move on to Tinian and Guam to take over the rest of the Mariana Islands.

After a flawless and successful invasion, the Americans seized the islands, which was the beginning of the end for the Japanese military and civilians. Saipan had been under the control of Japan since 1920. They knew they were defeated. For the American military, control over Saipan opened the way to the Japanese home islands, which were only 1,300 miles away. With this victory, Saipan became the launch point to retake the other islands in the Mariana chain. Now, the United States had an airbase from which bombers could strike the heart of the Japanese Empire. The Mariana campaign was referred to as *Operation Forager,* and it was during this campaign that the Seabees made one of their most important contributions in the Pacific Theater of Operations in the South Pacific.

With the support of naval bombardment, the soldiers had seized the island of Tinian within a week's time. The Seabees immediately went to work to construct the largest airbase of World War II, which covered the entire island. Months later, this airbase would be the launch base for the two B-29s, which would each carry and drop an atomic bomb on Japan, bringing the war to an end.

* * *

In October 1944, Dean was directly involved with building and operating the pontoon barges and causeways to allow the Allied Forces to come ashore onto the islands. He was present on the Philippine Island of Leyte when General MacArthur fulfilled his famous promise to return.

A final step toward the invasion of the Japanese home islands was to make the Philippines a major forward base in the Pacific. Thirty-seven thousand Seabees were spread around the important adjoining islands to build the facilities needed. By summer, the United States military forces prepared, and were ready for that final step to victory in the South Pacific.

* * *

On January 22, 1945, Dean and his crewmembers crossed the International Date Line. On that day he wrote a letter to Penny, and said, *When we get back, maybe I can tell you where I've been. Just get your map out and look at all the islands around the Equator, and you will know.*

* * *

After the fall of the Marianas islands, the Seabees worked day and night to build five large runways on the islands to be ready for the new B-29 bomber that carried ten tons of bombs with a 6,000-mile range. In March of 1945, there were 325 B-29s on the runways. The factory workers on the home front pumped out airplanes at a record pace.

The last big operation that would involve the Seabees was to seize Okinawa. On Easter Sunday, April 1, 1945, the forces landed on Okinawa's west coast beaches. Several Naval Construction Battalions participated in the operation, and provided pontoons for the landing. They built an entire base, which included ocean ports, roads, and bomber and fighter fields. Nearly 55,000 Seabees participated in the Okinawa construction operations. The fight for the island was long and hard, and didn't end until June 21, 1945.

By the summer of 1945, American military forces were ready for the last step on the road to victory in the South Pacific. During the summer, another plan was in the works. The *USS Indianapolis* arrived at Tinian from the Naval Weapons Center at Port Chicago, California. Its cargo was the top-secret components of an atomic bomb. The Seabees were there to help unload it, and store it in a shed they had built specifically for the mysterious weapon. They organized a detachment to guard the shed. Then scientists arrived to assemble the weapon while inside the shed along with the assistance of the Seabees. All that remained, was the order to load it on to a B-29.

## Chapter 12

It was July 13, 1945. Penny answered the door to the Western Union man who handed her a telegram from Dean. She held her breath for a moment. Was this good news or bad? She had received other telegrams from her husband since he had gone away. Each time she saw the Western Union man walking up to her doorstep with a telegram in hand, she worried what news it carried. This one brought the best news of all. Dean was coming home.

"WESTERN UNION
Collect = San Francisco Calif…1945 JUL 13 PM 12 40
MRS R D MESSINGER
217 SOUTH JEFFERSON ST APT 3

MEET ME IN PORTLAND BUS DEPOT SATURDAY
TWO OCLOCK
JULY 14TH
DEAN."

Dean's official separation from the U.S. Naval Service was November 27, 1945, but he was able to go home in July. He had been gone nearly two years. Their daughter was a baby when he left, now she was over two years old. Dean had written in his letter of May 19, 1945,

*Thanks for the lock of baby's hair – it looks like it ought to be*

*pretty. Honey, what do you think her reactions to me will be? Will she make up with me or will she be scared for a while? I'm afraid she won't want to have anything to do with me....*

*All my love to you both, Dean.*

Penny reflected back, "It was a long, lonesome time. It was a rough time."

The love of her life had returned, and they were husband and wife again. They had put their lives on hold, and now they were ready to pick up where they left off and be a family again. But there would be adjustments. Penny had been on her own for nearly two years. She learned how to manage her life, and earning her own money was liberating. The young girl her husband left behind had transformed into a confident, independent woman.

Dean returned as a young man who had seen what a young American man was not meant to see. He was worldly, mature beyond his years, and possessed a deep inner strength. The couple had changed, but distance and time had not changed their love for each other. Their love endured, and it was as strong as it was when he left.

The war was winding down, so Dean didn't expect to be called back. The country and world had already celebrated the surrender of Germany on May 8th that year, referred to as V-E Day (Victory in Europe Day). Japan was on the defensive, and couldn't last many more months, even though the Emperor of Japan and his generals refused to believe it.

* * *

The Japanese continued to suffer massive casualties and destruction, but refused to surrender. *Operation Downfall*, the invasion of Japan, was scheduled for November 1, 1945, to be led by General MacArthur. It was predicted that the invasion could cost over one million American lives and over ten million Japanese lives. While MacArthur was planning the invasion, President Truman, who had recently taken the reins when President Roosevelt died, was planning the final act of war, hoping to save millions of lives. He approved the use of two atomic bombs to be dropped on two key cities in Japan.

* * *

On August 6th, the weapon was loaded onto the B-29, the *Enola Gay,* and took off from the Tinian's North Field to drop the first bomb, nicknamed *Little Boy,* on the city of Hiroshima. Sixteen hours later, President Truman demanded Japan's surrender, with a warning that if they didn't comply, "They should expect a rain of ruin from the air, the like of which has never been seen on this earth." The Emperor of Japan refused. Three days later, on August 9th, a B-29, *Bock's Car,* flew from the Tinian runway, carrying the second bomb, called *Fat Man,* and dropped it on the city of Nagasaki. Over 140,000 Japanese civilians died either instantly or over time from the radiation poisoning. With such devastation, the Japanese leaders surrendered. The official surrender took place on September 2, 1945, on the battleship, *Missouri*. With Germany's surrender on May 8th, the long hard war was over.

* * *

Dean was proud to have been a member of the Naval Construction Battalion as a Seabee. The Seabees served on four continents and more than three hundred islands. Although their role was to fight to defend what they constructed, the Seabees performed many acts of heroisms. They were men who built and fought alongside American soldiers to keep America free, and witnessed the horrors and carnage of war they would never forget. Dean and his Battalion participated in some of the most important strategic moments during the war.

Dean was awarded the Asiatic-Pacific Area Campaign Medal, the Philippine Liberation Medal, the World War II Victory Medal, the American Area Campaign Medal, and a Presidential Unit Citation.

The training and experience he absorbed as a Seabee would follow him into civilian life, and take him worldwide in later years.

Dean and Penny witnessed the end of the war together.

On August 14, 1945, they hovered over their radio and listened to an announcement of breaking news from President Truman about Japan's surrender. He spoke at a press conference from the White House,

"This is the day we have been waiting for since Pearl Harbor. This is the day when Fascism finally dies, as we knew it would."

The whole world cried and cheered together. The citizens of the United States and the Allied nations felt an enormous sense of relief and unbounded joy. Two million Americans united in New York Times Square and watched fifteen thousand flash bulbs light up on the Times Tower flash the words "Official—Truman announces Japanese surrender." Those five words ignited ecstatic cheering and celebration. Church bells rang, and fireworks lit the sky. People danced, sang and drank, and strangers kissed strangers. The boys were coming home.

Dean and Penny served their country for close to two years—Dean as a fighting Seabee overseas, and Penny as a production soldier in the Boeing plant.

# Chapter 13

Now Americans were approaching the dawn of peace. Life was returning to normal, and the economy was growing stronger. When the soldiers came home, they resumed the jobs they left behind, or found a new peacetime job. Instead of war equipment, the industry produced goods to make the new *normal* life better.

The demand for the American home front to provide equipment, supplies and food for the war effort lifted the nation out of the Depression, and brought the return of prosperity. As the growth continued into the postwar era, the country emerged as the economic superpower of the world.

The world became a better place. Ironically, the countries that were affected by the war experienced an economic boom. The boom was considered an *economic miracle*. By the 1960s, Japan, which was the hardest hit because of the two atomic bombs, became the world's second largest economy after the United States.

It was hard to imagine that such a long, brutal and bloody war with so many lives lost, could have resulted in such a robust transformation for the United States and the rest of the world.

* * *

Dean and Penny resumed living in Kelso, Washington, and found a small house to rent. Penny worked part-time as a waitress in a family restaurant in Kelso. Dean's former employer, Hart Construction, held his job for him to resume upon his return from the war. Over time, Dean became the general supervisor.

The Messingers worked hard and saved their money, and it wasn't long before the couple bought their first home. They embraced the American dream.

Like so many of their fellow Americans, Dean and Penny contributed to the dramatic surge in the birthrate shortly after World War II ended. In a little over nine months after Dean returned home from the war, Penny gave birth to their son, Ron, on May 20, 1946. Before the war, the birthrate had gone down. When the servicemen came home, the size of the families grew. The *Greatest Generation* produced the *Baby Boomer* generation--babies born between 1946 and 1964. The year 1946 brought more babies into the world than ever before. The boomer generation comprised nearly forty percent of the population in the United States.

* * *

The Messingers were now a family of four and needed more square footage. After moving twice, they found a large house located in the hilltop suburb of Columbia Heights overlooking the city of Longview. They loved their new home.

Both Carol Ann and Ron, have memories of the big garden their father planted. Even though the neighbors told Dean no one had ever been able to grow a garden up there, he was determined to have a garden. They didn't have a lot of money at the time, and he thought a garden would save on the food bill. According to Ron, his father went a little overboard and planted more produce than they could consume. Dean ended up feeding a couple of neighbors as well.

Ron was quite young during their garden days. He shared about one of his favorite childhood pastimes in the garden. Ron said, "I liked to disappear into the tomato patch with my little Morton salt shaker to eat the sun-kissed tomatoes that were ready to harvest." He laughs about how his parents called out to him wondering where he was. "I loved those *hot* tomatoes," he said.

Carol Ann remembers the fun of crawling inside the *pole bean tents.* Dean had arranged poles into a teepee framework for the beans, which the sprawling vines quickly covered.

* * *

By now, Penny worked for the Longview Fibre Company in the Accounting Department. She enjoyed the idea of being socially active in the community. She joined Altrusa International of Cowlitz County, a group with a mission statement committing to make a difference in its community, country and the world. Penny was a member of Altrusa for several years.

She recalled an overseas trip the Altrusa group took to visit England, Scotland, Ireland, France and Italy. When they were in Nettuno, Lazio, Italy, Penny visited the large beautifully landscaped Sicily-Rome American Cemetery & Memorial, located near the famous Anzio beachhead. It was created to honor the American soldiers, sailors and civilians who participated in the Invasion of Italy. At the entrance of the cemetery, Penny admired a broad pool with a small island and cenotaph in the center made of Roman travertine. It was flanked with tall Italian cypress and colorful flowers, which were meticulously manicured. Just beyond the entrance, was the breath-taking sight of 7,861 headstones of the fallen heroes spread over gentle green slopes of lawn.

Penny shared a special experience. "I remembered the name of a family in Kelso who lost their son in Italy during World War II. So I wondered if he was buried there, and checked some names, and I actually found their son. I wanted to honor him so I bought some flowers from the floral shop that was on the premises, and placed the flowers on his grave and said a little prayer. When I returned home from our trip, I called his mother and told her I had found his grave, and put flowers on it. She was still a mother mourning her son. I had taken a picture of her son's grave and gave it to her. She was so touched. It takes such little things."

She also joined the Ladies' Elks in Kelso. During one of her meetings, one of the women in the group mentioned she was moving, and asked Penny if she would be interested in buying the Dairy Queen franchise in Kelso. Penny's love for ice cream went way back. She was smitten with the idea, and went home and asked her husband, "How would you like to own a Dairy Queen?" Dean knew it was a big gamble, but agreed. The youngest member of the family, Ron, had only one response, "Wow, I'm going to have a lot of ice cream to eat!"

Penny had been working at the Longview Fibre Company for about a year when they purchased the original Kelso Dairy Queen, which was located on the corner of 3rd and Vine. She hired people for the day shift so she could continue to work at Fibre, and work the night shift at the Dairy Queen. Finally, at the end of her second year at Fibre, she quit, and worked alone from opening to closing time at the Dairy Queen. Dean and Penny hired a babysitter to care for eight-year-old Carol Ann and five-year-old Ron during the daytime. At night, after coming home from work, Dean took over. Each night, he fed the children and read to them until they fell asleep. Then he rushed down to the Dairy Queen to help Penny close. Penny put in many long hours before she was able to hire any help.

Since Columbia Heights sat high above Longview, commuting down the steep hill from their home during the wintertime was difficult and dangerous. Around 1952, they decided to move into town where they would be closer to their Dairy Queen business and the children's schools. Carol Ann and Ron were able to walk to school.

Before long, Carol Ann was old enough to help her mother at the Dairy Queen. Both she and her brother have a vivid memory about their mother and silver dollars. Silver dollars were more common in the 1950s, and every time someone paid with a silver dollar, Penny kept it and exchanged it out. Then she put the silver dollars into savings, which accumulated fast enough to pay for their annual summer vacation. The family went to Canada, Mexico, California, Utah, and Yellowstone Park. The parents believed in educating their children, so they made sure to always visit a state capital and museum.

The Dairy Queen gamble in Kelso paid off, so Penny and Dean took a chance on a second Dairy Queen located in Longview that became available. Penny managed both Dairy Queens for several years. They had started out by offering only dairy products with a walk-up window. Eventually, Penny offered hamburgers and hotdogs.

She would become known as the Dairy Queen lady. There was a newspaper article written about her in the *Longview Daily News.*

The article headline read *Dairy Queen Owner is Progressive, Serves Community.*

*...Mrs. Messinger is that solid type of citizen whose fairness, friendliness and sincere desire to serve only the finest of hamburgers, ice cream and beverages prepared in a manner that leaves nothing to be asked for is accountable for a large measure of her success. As time goes on, her personal interests have become more closely interwoven with the business and civic affairs of the twin cities. As a result she has, quite naturally become accepted as a woman who can be called upon and who will cheerfully do her part to further the development of those community activities to which she is best fitted to lend assistance.*

*Priscilla Messinger has, by the conduct of The Dairy Queens and her attention to civic affairs, earned the friendship and good will of her fellow citizens. Mrs. Messinger is to be complimented for her activities and we of the Cowlitz County Advocate express the desire of her many friends, business associates and customers in wishing her continued success.*

Penny always said, "If you go to a Dairy Queen and order a cone, don't ever accept it if it doesn't have the curl on top."

* * *

Dean continued to work at Hart Construction for several years as a foreman. One of his jobs was to perform repairs and maintenance on the famed cantilever Longview Bridge, which spanned the Columbia River between Longview, Washington, and Rainier, Oregon.

In November of 1927, Congress had authorized private investors to construct the bridge. One of the investors was the founder of Longview, Robert Long (1850-1934). The bridge was specified to be 8,192 feet long with a clearance of 195 feet at mid span to accommodate tall-masted clipper ships, and would require more than 12,000 tons of steel. It was designed by the engineer of the famous Golden Gate Bridge in San Francisco, Joseph Baermann Straus (1870-1938). It officially opened in 1930 at the beginning of the Depression. Tolls were charged to help pay for the bridge. Finally, in 1947, the Washington State Toll Authority lifted the burden from the private investors and purchased it. By 1965, the bridge was debt free and the toll fees were eliminated. Later in 1980, the bridge was dedicated and renamed the Lewis & Clark Bridge in honor of the Lewis & Clark Expedition in 1805-1806.

Dean was proud of his contribution of labor on the bridge, but it nearly cost him his life. While working on the bridge, the scaffolding gave way, and Dean fell sixty feet and landed on a sand bar. He was rushed to the hospital, and although he had suffered a cracked vertebra at the base of his neck, he left the hospital the same day. Unfortunately, those who attended him hadn't detected his injury. He was fine until a small growth developed on the injury, which started pinching a nerve, and caused him to experience numbness in one of his legs. He underwent surgery wherein the surgeon scraped the growth off next to his spinal cord.

Penny recalled a moment when the family was crossing

the bridge.

"One day we were driving over the Lewis & Clark Bridge when the kids were little, Dad said, 'Ron, see that post there? I put that post in.' Ron's eyes opened wide. He was so proud, he told the kids at school later, 'My daddy built that bridge!' We got a chuckle out of that."

* * *

All was well with Dean's job until the owner died, and the son took over the company. The company didn't last long. Suddenly, Dean was out of work. Never one to waste any time, Dean began his search immediately. He heard about a bridge being built on the mouth of the Columbia River between Astoria, Oregon, and Point Ellice, Washington, and asked the DeLong Corporation about joining the crew. With his training and experience in the Seabees combined with his experience with Hart Construction, notably, his work on the Longview Bridge, the foreman didn't hesitate to hire him. The 4.1 mile long steel cantilever bridge was called the Astoria-Megler Bridge. It would become the longest continuous three-span through-truss bridge in the world. The bridge was needed to replace the ferry system, which couldn't keep up with the demand of crossing the river. The ferry crossed over ten miles of the waters of the Columbia and took thirty minutes. Construction of the bridge began on November 5, 1962, and Dean was there. After 1,356 days of construction, the governors of both states cut the ribbon to officially dedicate and open the Astoria-Megler Bridge on August 27, 1966. The bridge started out as a toll bridge to pay for the cost. Both Oregon and Washington states agreed to split the cost fifty/fifty. On December 24, 1993, two years ahead of schedule, the bridge bonds were paid off, and the tolls were removed. The bridge that had been dubbed the *Bridge to Nowhere* was a huge success.

In a short period of time, it became obvious Dean knew what he was doing, and the head man put him in charge. His sterling performance drew the attention of the DeLong Company owner, who quickly offered Dean the position of Superintendent of Southeast Asia. The DeLong Company built piers, bridges, and other types of heavy construction. Dean would also oversee any machinery repairs needed on barge boats.

# Chapter 14

It was 1964. The Messingers' life was about to change dramatically. With Dean's job taking him to Southeast Asia, Penny and Dean would have to live apart for the next two years. Separated again. Penny reflected back on her marriage years, "I lived alone a lot throughout our marriage." While Carol Ann had left the nest and married, Ron still had two years remaining before graduating from high school. Penny stayed at home to be with her son.

For the next three years, Penny and Dean shared their lives through letters. They counted the weeks until Penny would be able to follow her husband overseas.

Finally, in 1967, the time had come for Penny to join her husband in Singapore, which was where his main office was located. Going overseas to live with her husband for an extended period of time meant Penny would have to give up her beloved Dairy Queen business. She sold the Dairy Queens, and flew to Singapore just before Christmas. Penny lived with Dean overseas off and on for the next fourteen years. Through the years in Southeast Asia, Dean's work took them to Vietnam, Cambodia, Thailand, Burma and West Malaysia.

When Dean met her at the Singapore airport, he arrived in a chauffeured company car. The chauffeur drove them to a beautiful furnished high-rise apartment set upon a hill overlooking the city. The company had made the arrangements for them.

Dean was able to stay with Penny from time to time. After

being apart for two years, Penny was grateful for every moment they were together. At least they weren't half a world apart anymore. Sometimes he worked nearby, but other times he traveled further away such as Vietnam, which was under two hours flying time from the Singapore airport. He spent two years building bridges in Vietnam during the war. Other times, he worked in Saudi Arabia.

Penny's way of living changed dramatically. The island city-state of Singapore, which was often labeled the *New York of South East Asia,* and also called the *Lion City,* the *Garden City* or the *Little Red Dot,* offered an ethnic tapestry of cultures and religions. She would be living among a blend of Malay, Chinese, Arab, Indian, and English people.

Penny described her life in Singapore.

"Our two-bedroom apartment was very nice. We had a wonderful balcony, which overlooked the city below. At night, the city lights were beautiful. I had my own *amah,* who was a Chinese woman we hired to perform all the domestic tasks. Once in a while I asked her to cook for us when Dean was there. She lived with us in the second bedroom.

"Living in Singapore was nice. I wasn't afraid to go out by myself. I enjoyed shopping in a variety of shops. I went to the hairdresser weekly. While one lady was working on my hair, there was a lady working on each hand, then my feet. I joined the American Club for Women where I could swim, dine out, or take a course in Chinese brush painting. I would go there at night to play cards, bridge or dominoes. I made a lot of new friends.

"I took a course in Chinese cooking where I found out American style Chinese food was unknown. Real Chinese cooking is out of this world. You eat forever with fourteen to seventeen courses.

"You learn two things about food there. If you're not sure what it is, don't ask—it's better not to know. And if you're uneasy about what you might be eating, don't chew. Just swallow and you'd get along pretty well.

"We had a neighbor from Australia who was the number one jockey of Southeast Asia. His wife and I frequented the horse races together. Horse racing was the most popular pastime in Singapore.

"One of my most memorable activities was the safari I went on through the Malaysian Nature Study Society. I was exhausted, but the beauty of the jungle made the trip worth the effort.

"The people in Singapore loved anything American, especially in fashion. Their fashion was a mixture of Chinese and Western style. The fabrics were gorgeous, and the seamstresses excellent, but there just wasn't the flair of American styling.

"And whenever I went somewhere to make a purchase, there was always the question, 'how much you pay?'

"I stayed busy in Singapore. Staying busy made it easier when Dean was gone. The *Lion City* was a very pleasant place to live."

Although Singapore was Penny and Dean's base, the couple moved to Bahrain in the Arabian Gulf where Dean had to work for several months. Penny didn't want to be separated from Dean for such a long period of time, so she went with him. She went twice for several months at a time. One time was close to a year.

"I went to Saudi Arabia where they didn't want women, and as a woman, you wouldn't want to be there. During those years, you had to be damn careful! You couldn't go out alone. If you did, you might not come back. We couldn't get a car there, and I didn't dare get in a cab because I didn't know whom I would end up with.

"With our Company, there were three wives, and we stuck together. For instance, if one of us needed to go out such as to the post office, we would call each other and arrange to go out together. I recall one time when I was standing in line at the post office, I suddenly felt a man's hands groping my derriere. It was shocking and scary, but I didn't dare turn and glare at him because it would be made to appear that it was my fault.

"We hired a very dependable house boy who did the housework, and cooking, if I asked. He cared about my safety. If I mentioned about going to a certain place, he would say, 'Don't go there, ma'am.'

"It was also hotter than heck, and most places didn't have air conditioning. I didn't enjoy my time there."

Before leaving Saudi Arabia, Penny trekked across the dunes of the Dubai Desert on the back of a camel. It didn't take her long to get used to the rhythm of the camel. The trek was peaceful, but exciting at the same time, and the ocean of sand was awe-inspiring.

"There were times in the future when Dean would have to return to Saudi Arabia for a long period of time, and would be living on the barge boats. We decided I was better off staying in Singapore, or at home in the States. Sometimes Dean would be gone for six months at a time. There weren't many wives who chose to live in Saudi Arabia."

* * *

Dean also worked for the Raymond International Company. His job took them to Spain where they lived for a year.

"We had an apartment on the northern end of the beautiful Costa Del Sol, overlooking the Mediterranean Sea," said Penny.

Penny enjoyed living in Spain, and even went to a bullfight.

Once, she entertained visitors from her hometown of Kelso, and took them to Gibraltar. Gibraltar shares its northern border with Spain, and Tangier, Morocco, and for centuries has been known as Europe's gateway to Africa. Penny booked them on the most popular ferry route, Algeciras to Tanger (Tangier), which took only thirty minutes to cross the Strait of Gibraltar to Morocco. "Everything was quite expensive, and very few people spoke English. The weather was comparable to San Diego, sunny and balmy most of the time."

# Chapter 15

The Messingers returned to Longview in early 1980, and purchased a beautiful condo overlooking the Cowlitz River. Dean continued to work locally, and also worked for the U.S. Army Corps of Engineers.

When Mount St. Helens erupted in the spring of 1980, it generated an avalanche of over three billion yards of sediment, which dumped into the Toutle River, and mud from the avalanche flowed into the Cowlitz River channel and the Columbia River. Penny and Dean had witnessed the eruption from their condo living room. As they watched the eruption, Dean knew he would be one of the responders to the disaster.

The U.S. Army Corps of Engineers responded, and initiated disaster cleanup assistance. In the following months after the eruption, the Corps constructed a sediment retention structure to offset the massive flow of debris that would go into the Toutle, Cowlitz, and Columbia Rivers. Dean and the other members of the Corps helped to provide flood risk reductions for the communities of Longview, Kelso, Castle Rock, and Lexington. Dean's own community of Longview was at risk.

Dean retired from the U.S. Army Corps of Engineers in 1985. Penny had not gone back to work after they returned from overseas. She and Dean stayed busy with activities. Although Dean had joined both the Kelso Masonic Lodge and the Longview-Kelso Elks in the 1950s, he resumed his activity to only the Longview-Kelso Elks.

Penny's main activity was and continues as a member of Maple Chapter Order of the Eastern Star, for which she has served as Worthy Matron several times, as well as holding a number of other offices. To date, 2017, she is a sixty-year member. The members are like an extended family to her.

In 1985, Penny added to her list of community groups by joining the Longview chapter of the Daughters of the American Revolution and held officer positions.

Penny and Dean enjoyed a quiet life together. They joined an RV Club. For awhile, they travelled with their RV across the nation. Penny said, "I have always enjoyed traveling, but it can get old. It was nice to be finally settled."

* * *

Dean and Penny raised both of their children in Longview.

Carol Ann graduated from high school in 1961, married in 1962, and moved to Alaska where she raised her six children. She divorced her husband in 1983, and eventually met and married Ross Power. Carol Ann and Ross moved back to Longview in 2012 to be near her parents.

Ron graduated from the same high school as Carol Ann in 1965, and married in 1966. He and his wife settled in Utah and raised their family there. During the Vietnam War, he was drafted. Years later, he served in the Air Force for four years. Next, he joined the National Guard. After the September 11th attack, Ron was called up to go to Afghanistan. After he returned home, he went back to the desert for two years. The children had left the nest, so his wife was alone. Ron knew it was hard on her. Their oldest son moved in to help his mother until Ron returned. Ron could relate to his own mother being left alone while his father was overseas in World War II.

# Chapter 16

On one of my interview meetings with Penny, Carol Ann announced, "I have a wonderful idea. Let's take mom on a road trip back to her hometown." I replied that it was a great idea. Penny hadn't been back to her roots since 1940. Carol Ann went into action and planned the trip.

During the planning process, she contacted Kelly Calhoun, Executive Director/Curator, Museum of the North Beach, and Lee Marriott, President, Moclips by the Sea Historical Society & Museum of the North Beach. She briefed them about our plan for the three of us to visit the areas where Penny grew up—Aloha, Moclips and Pacific Beach. The museum was a key place to visit since it possesses an impressive collection of local photographs, oral stories, newspaper articles and interviews.

Kelly and Lee were most receptive to the idea, and welcomed us with warm hospitality. Since the trip was a three-hour drive one way, we knew we would need to spend the night. Kelly and Lee pulled some strings, and were able to offer us a beach house to stay overnight at no charge. The following morning, they planned to take us to breakfast at the beautiful Ocean Crest Resort.

The date was set for our adventure together.

# Chapter 17

It was Monday, September 18, 2017, the day we were driving to Penny's hometown. Carol Ann and Penny met me at my house at 9:00 a.m. I drove separately to give us more room in our cars. Each of us filled our backseats with an assortment of wraps and overnight bags. With full tanks of gas, we were on our way.

About midway, we stopped for a break in the town of Raymond, and found a cafe for a light snack. Since Penny had celebrated her 95th birthday four days earlier, I presented her with a birthday gift, a purple and green enamel pin with a pewter clasp. Penny loved it, and said, "I shall wear it proudly." She wore it on both days of our trip. I knew she loved purple, and the green looked great with her now-tinted copper colored hair. After we each ate our slice of French Toast, we were on our way again.

We arrived at our destination around noon. The building, which the museum occupies, was the former *Hewitt's Frozen Foods* grocery store and *Flying A* gas station. Kelly was waiting for us. He had already laid out a plethora of information that pertained to Penny. He had even brought out the 1940 yearbook from the high school where Penny graduated—Moclips High School. Penny signed it, and I snapped a picture. Penny and Carol Ann, in return, brought several pictures and documents that Penny had saved over the years to donate to the museum. Kelly was especially pleased with the class pictures taken at the two-room schoolhouse in Aloha.

Penny had kept almost every year through school beginning with the first grade in Aloha.

Museum of the North Beach
*Courtesy of the Museum of the North Beach*

Priscilla with Kelly and Lee in front of the museum

Priscilla with Kelly in the Museum holding a picture of her hometown of Aloha

Priscilla in the museum holding her 1940 Moclips High School yearbook

At 2:00 p.m., we followed Kelly to a house in Aloha to meet two ladies who wanted to meet Penny, and wondered if she had known any of their family. They were pleased to learn that Penny did remember some of their family members. It was nice to watch the two generations connect.

Next, they drove us to the Aloha Lumber Company millsite, which had once been an active lumber mill and town. It is now a ghost town. What a shock to see a once thriving town completely deserted and reduced to shambles.

While we had been at the museum, I had seen pictures of Aloha when Penny lived there. Only a handful of buildings are still standing, and they are beyond saving. They sit vacant and have greyed with age. The general store is still there, but very little else. It closed in 1965. The store was the hub of the mill town. The lumber mill was situated behind it. We drove around back for a better look. Now, the millsite is a skeleton with remnants of the past lying still. I saw huge logs, greyed with age, with a diameter that would be impossible to find now, and stacks of old lumber also greyed with age.

Penny's house would have been near the mill. There were two streets, Front Street and Back Street. Penny lived on Front Street. Presently, the streets are only grass-covered paths, and it takes some imagination to visualize all the houses that were once neatly lined up in a row on the two streets. Each house was numbered. We learned from the site map, that Penny's house was number thirteen, and sat on the end, and the bunkhouse for the loggers sat adjacent to it. Aloha Hall had occupied the building of the former Aloha Elementary School. The Hall was the place to go for the Saturday night dances with live music. It was used for the locals to hold parties, Christmas and Thanksgiving dinners, and also as a voting place.

As we had hoped, being on location triggered much of Penny's memories. After all, it's been seventy-seven years since Penny graduated from high school, married the same year, and shortly thereafter moved to the Longview/Kelso area where she lives now. As we stood on the site, Penny began to describe exactly where her house sat and pointed in the direction where Moclips High School was located a few minutes away. Presently, there is one center section of the facade of the school still standing.

Across the main road from the millsite, two buildings still stand. One was the Aloha Tavern, which Penny insisted was called the pool hall, where all the kids hung out, and next to it, is a building that was once the post office. The post office began operation in 1906. The three-story hotel, now gone, sat west of the pool hall.

Between looking at the site map back at the museum and Penny's descriptions, I could visualize what the lumber town was like in its heyday. I could see people going in and out of the general store. I could see where the railroad tracks ran through the town and on to the timber site. I could see the where the speeder brought Penny's injured father from the woods. When he was rushed to the Hoquiam Hospital, he most likely would have been taken in Aloha's first ambulance, the *Blue Bomb,* which was an old Chevy Suburban. It was housed in a garage across from the pool hall/tavern.

The Aloha Lumber Company continued its operation for several decades, despite surviving many devastating fires and economic downturns. The mill was purchased by Evans Products in November 1964, and ultimately, closed for good.

Aloha Lumber Co., 1929
*Courtesy of the Museum of the North Beach*

Aerial view of Aloha, 1940s
*Courtesy of the Museum of the North Beach*

The Aloha General Store, present day 2017
*Courtesy of the Museum of the North Beach*

Remnants of Aloha Lumber Co., present day 2017
*Courtesy of the Museum of the North Beach*

Remnants of the mill, present day 2017
*Courtesy of the Museum of the North Beach*

* * *

After we finished visiting the Aloha site, we went back to the museum. There were two ladies waiting who were anxious to meet Penny and exchange information, Ruth Gangwish and Barbara Baker.

Ruth grew up in Aloha, and worked four years for Aloha Lumber, then left in 1965. Eleven years ago, she collaborated with the writer, Richard Sterling, to create the book, *Aloha Lumber Company*. Ruth's mother, Pearl A. Moore, was appointed postmaster for Aloha in March of 1963 until the Aloha post office closed in April 1979.

Barbara has lived in the area for over sixty years. She was in possession of a full diary written during World War II by Charles H. Baker. She shared an entry written about Penny's brother, Myron.

They mentioned the names of many of the original families in the area, and Penny knew about some of them. They were excited to meet an early resident of Aloha.

After several hours of historical exploration, Kelly led us to the charming two-bedroom beach house we would be staying in, located at Moclips near Pacific Beach. As soon as I stepped out of the car, I inhaled the sea air and listened to the rolling waves. The wind coming off the ocean blew my hair, and I didn't mind a bit. The ocean beach was out of sight, but reachable within walking distance.

When we drove down the little road called Railroad Avenue, we noticed a single caboose parked alongside the road. We asked Kelly and Lee about it. They explained that it was the 1910 Northern Pacific Railroad caboose from the last train to Moclips. The seaside town was the furthest point west of the entire North Pacific line. When the Northern Pacific train rolled into Moclips, the townspeople heard the whistle as it approached it destination, the Pacific Railroad Depot. The depot was built in 1905, and torn down in the 1950s. Tracks are no longer there. They were torn up from Moclips to Hoquiam in the early 1980s. The caboose now sits on the original 1904 Northern Pacific Railroad grade. Through a great deal of effort, the Historical Society now owns the caboose and had it moved from where it sat seven blocks away on Beach Lane.

The 1910 Northern Pacific Railroad caboose sitting on Railroad Avenue, present day 2017

Then Kelly and Lee pointed toward the ocean where the three-story Moclips Beach Hotel once stood. It sat only twelve feet from the ocean, and was a block long. Being so close to the ocean led to its demise because of a series of fatal storms beginning in 1911. The storms not only took out the hotel, but most of the town as well.

The hotel began as one man's dream. When Dr. Lycan learned the Northern Pacific Railroad would be building a spur from Hoquiam to Moclips, he announced about his plan to build a hotel at the beach. In 1905, the original two-story hotel had one hundred and fifty rooms, and sat thirty-six feet from the ocean. But, four months after the hotel opened, a fire destroyed it.

Refusing defeat, Dr. Lycan invested his life's fortune, and built a much larger hotel, which boasted three hundred and twenty-five rooms with two hundred and seventy of the rooms facing the incredible ocean view. Rather than repeat the L-shape design of the first hotel, he designed it as an E-shape. The grand lady was ready to greet her guests by 1907.

The Moclips Beach Hotel was advertised as a healthy getaway from city life. Dr. Lycan truly believed that Moclips by the sea was the place to be for health and pleasure. Sadly, he had only been able to live his dream for four years when three fatal storms in 1911, 1913, and 1914 destroyed his hotel. He watched his dream wash away. The doctor moved to Tenino, Washington, and died in December of 1912. Lee Marriott said, "Dr. Lycan died of a broken heart." A bronze historical marker called *A Broken Dream* is located at the intersection of Pacific Avenue and 4th near the beach.

There we were, standing where throngs of wealthy people had once arrived on the Northern Pacific train to enjoy Pacific Beach and the Moclips Beach Hotel.

I rolled my mind back in time. I could visualize it all. The train chugged in and stopped at the depot allowing its wealthy passengers, dressed in their traveling finery, to disembark. The hotel was a short walk away. They breathed the moist salt air and felt the breeze brush their skin, the same as us one hundred and ten years later. They checked into the grand Moclips Beach Hotel for a healthy getaway from city life. The train and hotel brought life to the area, and soon a thriving resort town evolved. Everything was in walking distance for the visitors. Now, as I looked around, the town and hotel are gone. The once bustling resort town has become a neighborhood of modest beach houses. How devastated Dr. Lycan must have been.

The Moclips Beach Hotel, 1907
*Courtesy of the Museum of the North Beach*

The Moclips Beach Hotel after the three fatal storms, 1911, December 1913, January 1914
*Courtesy of the Museum of the North Beach*

* * *

We unpacked our cars and settled in. Carol Ann and I had put together a nice picnic supper, which we pulled out of our ice chests. I had brought a bottle of peach sparkling wine along with wine glasses. Albeit, the glasses were plastic, but at least they were the right shape. The three of us clicked our glasses and toasted to our successful trip and our friendship. I had gained some insightful information, Penny relived the early years of her past, and Carol Ann learned more about her mother's history. Best of all, we felt we had made new friends at the museum.

After supper, we all retired to our bedrooms and crashed.

The following morning, Kelly and Lee arrived to take us to breakfast at the Ocean Crest Resort. The view of the ocean was spectacular, and so was the meal. It was gourmet.

During breakfast, Kelly and Lee announced exciting news about their future plans for the museum. The Historical Society will be partnering with the North Beach community to rebuild the train depot three blocks from the current location, which will become the new home for the museum. The Ocean Crest company owns the building, which the museum is presently occupying. Once the museum is in its new home, the Ocean Crest owners will retrofit the old grocery store building to open a gift store and art gallery. The resort is walking distance from the Museum's new building, so it will work out well.

When we finished the enjoyable breakfast, Kelly and Lee drove us back to the beach house.

Breakfast at the Ocean Crest Resort
Seated at the table beginning on the left going clockwise: Lee Marriott (President, Moclips by the Sea Historical Society & Museum of the North Beach), Priscilla (Penny) Dean Messinger, Lilly Robbins Brock (Author), Carol Ann Power (Priscilla's daughter), and Kelly Calhoun (Executive Director/Curator, Museum of the North Beach).

With a long drive back home ahead of us, we thanked Kelly and Lee for their generous hospitality and said goodbye. We also left a thank you gift and note for the owners of the house. Everyone had been so generous to us.

Finally, we loaded up our cars, locked up the house, and headed home. We drove back on the beautiful Hidden Coast Scenic Byway SR 109, which passes by charming oceanfront towns. I could barely keep my eyes on the road as I drove past one ocean scene after another framed by wind-sculptured evergreens.

We all arrived home before dark as planned. It was a good trip, especially for Penny to go back home after seventy-seven years.

# Chapter 18

Present day in this year of 2017, Penny and Carol Ann live together. In 2015, both Penny and Carol Ann lost the love of their lives—their husbands. It was a tragic year for the Messinger family. First, in February, Carol Ann lost her husband, Ross. Then in April, Penny lost Dean, her high school sweetheart. She and Dean were in their 75th year of marriage. For Carol Ann, it was a double blow. She lost both her husband and father in less than two months' time.

* * *

Penny and Dean had been together for a lifetime. They grew up side by side from high school on through all the trials and tribulations of their era. They were part of the *Greatest Generation*—a generation of strength, perseverance, and courage. Each of them served their country. Dean overseas, and Penny on the home front. Like so many married couples during the war, they didn't hesitate to put their married lives on hold. Their country came first. Penny spoke about Dean with the greatest love in her voice, and said, "It was a good marriage. No marriage problems. He was a good provider. I miss him terribly."

* * *

Neither Penny nor Carol Ann wanted to live alone, so Carol Ann moved in with Penny. It's a win-win arrangement. They share in the household duties. Carol Ann does the cooking, and Penny cleans. They each have their own pet. Penny has a cat, which she adores, and Carol Ann has a Poodle that has been her faithful companion for fifteen years.

Penny still likes to get her hair styled. Refusing to allow her hair to be grey, she has it tinted in her signature copper color. Carol Ann faithfully drives her there or anywhere else she would like to go. On their way home from town, they usually stop at the local Dairy Queen to enjoy a hot fudge sundae, Penny's all-time favorite.

Presently, Penny is a grandmother to ten grandchildren, thirteen great grandchildren, and one great-great grandchild. She also has two step grandchildren, four great step grandchildren, and one great-great step grandchild.

Quite a legacy for the Messinger family.

Priscilla (Penny) Dean Messinger, December 2017

# ACKNOWLEDGMENTS

It was a pleasure to meet and interview Priscilla Dean Messinger. She was one of the many Rosie the Riveters during World War II doing their part to help win the war. I would like to thank her for allowing me to write about her life. I was honored when she handed me her high school diary revealing the private thoughts of a young girl. The diary had remained closed since 1940. She also allowed me to read the private letters written to her from her husband while he served in World War II.

Many thanks go to Priscilla's daughter, Carol Ann. She was extremely helpful and supportive. It was she who dug through boxes of pictures and memorabilia to help me piece together Priscilla's life.

I would like to thank Priscilla's son, Ron Messinger, for granting me interview time. He was most helpful.

A special thank you goes to two of my Mary Richardson Walker Chapter D.A.R. sisters, Diana Justice and Judy Sapirstein, who approached me with the idea of meeting Priscilla and writing her story.

Thank you to Kelly Calhoun, Executive Director/Curator, Museum of the North Beach, and Lee Marriott, President, Moclips by the Sea Historical Society & Museum of the North Beach Museum (**www.moclips.org**). They were gracious hosts to Priscilla, Carol Ann, and myself during our visit to Priscilla's hometown. Throughout the process, there were times when I asked for certain historical information and pictures, and they didn't to hesitate to respond to my inquiries.

As always, my family deserves a heartfelt thank you for their support. My husband, Phil, and my sister, June, were early readers and proofreaders. I can always count on my daughter Alecia to apply her masterful editing skills to my manuscript.

My daughter Vivi Anne continues to work by my side utilizing her skills and talent to format the book, and to design and create the book cover.

A thank you also goes to my sister-in-law Merrily Graham who always cheers me on.

# REFERENCES

## Prologue

"The Willow Run Bomber Plant: Save a Piece of History." Save The Willow Run Bomber Plant, www.savethebomberplant.org/save-a-piece-of-history/.

"Land Cleared for Ford's Willow Run Plant."History.com, A&E Television Networks, www.history.com/this-day-in-history/land-cleared-for-fords-willow-run-plant.

## Chapter 2

"HistoryLink.org." President Franklin Roosevelt tours the Olympic Peninsula on October 1, 1937. - HistoryLink.Org, www.historylink.org/File/5434.

Finn J.D. John – January 27, 2012, and Downloadable audio file (MP3, 96 Kbps). "Radical Wobblies found support among Oregon loggers." Offbeat Oregon History: Album cover art, offbeatoregon.com/1301d-wobblies-come-to-oregon-timber.html.

"Homesteading This Dry Land." State Information Technology Services

Division. http://svcalt.mt.gov/education/textbook/chap ter13/Chapter13.pdf

**Chapter 3**

"HistoryLink.org." President Franklin Roosevelt tours the Olympic Peninsula on October 1, 1937. - HistoryLink.Org, www.historylink.org/File/5434.

**Chapter 7**

"Anti-Japanese Organizations." After Internment Japanese American's Right to Return, depts.washington.edu/civilr/after_internment.htm.

National Veterans Network (NVN), www.nationalveteransnetwork.com/100.shtml.

"The Purple Heart Battalion." World book, 4 May 2017, www.worldbook.com/behind-the-headlines/The-Purple-Heart-Battalion.

"Nisei." Monte Cassino Battlefield Tours,montecassinotours.com/index.php/page/id/6/nis ei.html

**Chapter 9**

Intro | OSU Press, osupress.oregonstate.edu/book/cohassett-beach-chronicles/intro.

History.com Staff. "The U.S. Home Front During World War II." History.com, A&E Television Networks, 2010, www.history.com/topics/world-war-ii/us-home-front-during-world-war-ii.

Yellin, Emily. Our Mothers' War: American Women at Home and at the Front During World War II. Free Press, 2005.

**Chapter 11**

Trauntvein, Myrna Rae. "Grammy's Gleanings." More About Seabees and My Dad, 1 Jan. 1970, grammysgleanings.blogspot.com/2011/12/more-about-seabees-and-my-dad.html.

Battle of Saipan - The Final Curtain, David Moore, www.battleofsaipan.com/seabee.htm.

"D-Day in the Pacific – the invasion of Saipan." WWII Today RSS, ww2today.com/15-june-1944-d-day-in-the-pacific-invasion-of-saipan.

History.com Staff. "Battle of Saipan." History.com, A&E Television Networks,
2009, www.history.com/topics/world-war-ii/battle-of-saipan.

**Chapter 12**

History.com Staff. "V-J Day." History.com, A&E Television Networks, 2009, www.history.com/topics/world-war-ii/v-j-day.

**Chapter 13**

"HistoryLink.org." Longview Bridge (Later renamed Lewis and Clark Bridge) spanning the Columbia River opens on March 29, 1930. -

HistoryLink.Org, www.historylink.org/File/5411.

Topinka, 2003 Lyn. The Columbia River - Astoria-Megler Bridge, Oregon, columbiariverimages.com/Regions/Places/astoria_megle r_bridge.html.

"Astoria Megler Bridge." Visit Long Beach Peninsula, 19 Apr. 2014, funbeach.com/astoria-megler-bridge/.

**Chapter 15**

Portland District, www.nwp.usace.army.mil/About/Current-projects/Mount-St-Helens-EIS/.

**Chapter 17**

"Moclips." Moclips – Travel guide at Wikivoyage, en.wikivoyage.org/wiki/Moclips.

"A dream washed away." BANNER, washingtoncoastmagazine.com/2017/05/a-dream-washed-away/.

Wolford, Matthew. Aloha Lumber Company, www.trestlewalker.com/AlohaLCo.html.

# AUTHOR'S NOTE TO READERS

~ Thank you for reading *Victory on The Home Front*. I hope you enjoyed it. If so, I would be very grateful if you could take a moment to leave a review on the book's Amazon page. It can be as brief as you like.

~ Visit my website: lillyrobbinsbrock.com

Thank you so much,

Lilly

# AUTHOR BIO

Lilly Robbins Brock and her husband live in a quiet country setting on the shores of the Columbia River in Cathlamet, Washington.

She began her business as an interior designer in 1980, and has recently retired. Living in the country is the ideal environment for Lilly to pursue her lifelong desire to write. She also enjoys gardening, and realized her pioneer family's planter blood is alive and well within her. Her book, *Food Gift Recipes From Nature's Bounty* was inspired by the garden and orchard. Preserving the food evolved into the idea of sharing some of that food—the gift of food.

Lilly loves history and one of her passions has been

researching the genealogy of her family. She was born and raised in Olympia, Washington where her pioneer family homesteaded in the late 1800s. She has been working on a historical fiction novel, *Intrepid Journey,* about a family in the 1850s traveling on a paddle wheel steamship from New York to the rugged Pacific Northwest via the dangerous South American route. It's a revealing glimpse into the past of what life was like at that time.

Her book, *Intrepid Journey,* was put on hold when she discovered two letters written by her now deceased father while he was on the battlefront of World War II. The letters inspired her to find a World War II veteran still living and tell his story. She found her veteran and wrote *Wooden Boats & Iron Men* to honor him and all veterans. She recently finished her second book about another World War II veteran, *Ever A Soldier*. He turned one hundred years old in July 2017.

Lilly feels that every veteran has a story, and at least she has been able to shine a light on these two extraordinary men.

Now she is shining a light on the women who contributed to the war effort during World War II, and has written about a *Rosie the Riveter,* now ninety-five years old, in her latest book, *Victory on the Home Front.*

To stay tuned in to current and upcoming projects, please feel free to visit www.lillyrobbinsbrock.com, or if you have any questions or comments, you may contact her at lilly@lillyrobbinsbrock.com.

Made in the USA
Columbia, SC
17 January 2018